AQA English Language and Literature

AS

Unit 2: Themes in language and literature

Exclusively endorsed by AQA

Marian Picton
Series editor
Chris Purple

Nelson Thornes

Published in 2012 by:
Nelson Thornes Ltd
Delta Place
27 Bath Road
CHELTENHAM
GL53 7TH
United Kingdom

12 13 14 15 16 / 10 9 8 7 6 5 4 3 2 1

A catalogue record for this book is available from the British Library

ISBN 978 1 4085 1555 6

Cover photograph by Tim MacPherson/Cultura/Corbis
Page make-up by Pantek Media, Maidstone

Printed and bound in China by 1010 Printing International Ltd

Acknowledgements
The author and the publisher would also like to thank the following for permission to reproduce material:

pp8, 32–3, 41, 42 *The Road of Wigan Pier* by George Orwell (Copyright © George Orwell, 1937); pp23, 47, 51, 68 Extracts from *Testament of Youth* by Vera Brittain are reproduced by permission of Mark Bostridge and T.J. Brittain-Catlin, Literary Executors for the Estate of Vera Brittain 1970; pp11 from *Ten Commandments of the Detective Novel* by Raymond Chandler. Copyright © Nicholas Parsons, 1985; pp12, 27–8, 36, 39–40, 55–6 *The Lady in the Lake* by Raymond Chandler. Copyright © Raymond Chandler, 1943. Reproduced by permission of the author's estate; pp10, 15, 16, 18 Reprinted by permission of HarperCollins Publishers Ltd © 1985 J.G Ballard; pp17 from *Alive! The Story of the Andes Survivor* by Piers Paul Read, published by Arrow Books. Reprinted by permission of The Random House Group Ltd; pp4, 17, 30, 34 from *Blood River* by Tim Butcher, published by Vintage Reprinted by permission of The Random House Group Ltd.

Every effort has been made to contact copyright holders and we apologise if any have been overlooked. Should copyright have been unwittingly infringed in this publication the owners should contact the publishers, who will make the correction at reprint.

Contents

Introduction to this book

Nelson Thornes and AQA

Nelson Thornes has worked in collaboration with AQA to ensure that this book offers you the best support for your AS or A Level course and helps you to prepare for your exams. The partnership means that you can be confident that the range of learning, teaching and assessment practice materials has been checked by the senior examining team at AQA before formal approval, and is closely matched to the requirements of your specification.

How to use this book

This book covers Unit 2 of the specification for your course and is arranged in a sequence approved by AQA. The book is divided into two sections; each section will prepare you for a certain type of question for assessment as coursework.

Unit 2 of your English Language and Literature course focuses on the coursework assignment. The first section of this book explores thematic links and stylistic differences between the paired set texts, focusing on preparing you for writing your analytical coursework piece (Part A). The second section provides guidance on your creative writing piece (Part B).

Definitions of all key terms and any words that appear in bold can be found in the glossary at the back of this book.

The features in this book include:

Learning objectives

At the beginning of each unit you will find a list of learning objectives that contain targets linked to the requirements of the specification.

Key terms

Terms that you will need to be able to define and understand. These terms are coloured blue in the textbook and their definitions also appear in the glossary at the end of this book.

Research point

Suggestions for further research to enhance your studies and develop the kind of thinking that will help you achieve the highest grades in your English Language and Literature B course.

Links

Links to other areas in the textbook, or in your experience from GCSE, which are relevant to what you are reading.

Further reading

Links to further sources of information, including websites and other publications.

Think about it

Short activities that encourage reflection.

Background information

In Unit 1, information that will inform your study of a particular Anthology text.

Practical activity

Activities to develop skills, knowledge and understanding that will prepare you for assessment in English Language and Literature B.

Critical response activity

Activities that focus on a specific extract to develop skills relevant to your assessment in the examination.

AQA Examiner's tip

Hints from AQA examiners to help you with your study and to prepare you for your coursework.

Commentary

Examples of answers you might give to the activities. These are designed to help you to understand what type of response the examiner is looking for, not to tell you the answer. There are many equally valid responses, so you will find this book most helpful if you try the activity yourself first and then look at the commentary to read another opinion. Not all activities have a commentary.

AQA examination questions are reproduced by permission of the Assessment and Qualifications Alliance.

Web links for this book

Because Nelson Thornes is not responsible for third-party content online, there may be some changes to this material that are beyond our control. In order for us to ensure that the links referred to are as up to date and stable as possible, please let us know at **webadmin@nelsonthornes.com** if you find a link that does not work and we will do our best to redirect these, or to list an alternative site.

Introduction to English Language and Literature

Integrated study of language and literature

The books in this series are designed to support you in your AS and A2 English Language and Literature studies. What is special about this subject is that it brings together aspects of two other kinds of A Level English course – the separate English Literature and English Language specifications – and there are real advantages in continuing your studies of English Language and Literature in an integrated course of this sort.

English at every level up to GCSE requires both language and literature to be studied as essential parts of the course. How can you study literature properly without being keenly interested in the medium of that literature – the ways in which words, sentences, paragraphs and chapters interrelate to create texts of various kinds? These texts may be novels, short stories, plays, documentary scripts, poems and non-fiction texts of a whole range of types and forms.

Being inquisitive about language in all of its forms and habitats is probably the most important quality that you can bring to your studies. We are immersed in language – it is our medium of communication with other people, it is the medium of entertainment (radio, television, comedy clubs, etc.) and a medium of instruction and information ('how to …' books, labels on medicines). More than that, my language and your language form essential parts of our identities, our individual personalities.

If you go on to study English at university, you will also encounter a subject which has largely abandoned sharp distinctions between 'literature' and 'language' study as unhelpful oversimplifications. You will inevitably be looking at how writers use language when you study a work of literature, and your knowledge about language and how it is used can help you to appreciate and understand how writers and speakers, readers and listeners can be creative and responsive in their experiences of language.

It is important not to think of A Level English Language and Literature as a mix-and-match course in which you 'do language' in one section of a unit and 'do literature' in another section. The point is that language study and literature study are integrated and you need to think about how your interest in language can extend and enhance your appreciation of literary texts. You also need to think about literary texts as examples of language being used in ways that repay close scrutiny, analysis and reflection. There are four main skills you need to develop during your AS and A2 course:

- You need to show that you are capable of reading texts closely and thoughtfully and writing about those texts in ways that show intelligent engagement and control.

- You need to show that you understand the characteristics of various kinds of spoken language, ranging from spontaneous exchanges between friends or strangers to carefully prepared speeches that are designed to persuade large numbers of people in live events or via television and radio.

- You need to show that you are capable of producing writing that is appropriate to the purpose and audience specified in the task, showing conscious control of your choices of vocabulary, grammar and structure.

Think about it

'Language most shows a man: speak that I may see thee.' *Ben Jonson*

- What do you think Jonson meant?

- Do you form an impression of a person from the way he speaks?

- Did Jonson intend his comment to apply to women, do you think? If so, why did he not refer to women as well as men?

- Does Jonson's comment also apply to the way men and women write?

You need to show that you are capable of writing in a focused and analytical way about your own writing – the processes you apply, the choices you make and the evaluation of whether the text works as well as you intended.

All of these activities build directly on the skills you have developed during your GCSE course and in your earlier secondary years, as well as in your primary school and during the pre-school years when you learned language skills by imitating adults and children with whom you grew up. These are skills that many of us continue to develop as the range of our experiences as readers, writers, speakers and listeners expands.

The units

This course focuses on a number of literary texts and on particular language topics. Here is a preview of each of the four units that make up the AS and A2 course.

Unit 1 (ELLB1): Introduction to language and literature study
Examination: 1 hour and 45 minutes

For this unit you will study an Anthology of thematically linked spoken and written texts. The Anthology covers the three main literary genres of prose fiction, poetry and drama as well as a range of non-literary texts. The theme for this Anthology (covering examinations in 2012, 2013 and 2014 only) is 'Food Glorious Food'. You will answer two questions, the first on an unseen text (or texts) which is thematically linked to the Anthology. The second question is set on the texts studied in the Anthology and will require you to comment on writers/speakers' uses of language and their attitudes towards a specified theme. This is an **open book examination**.

Unit 2 (ELLB2): Themes in language and literature
Coursework

The aim of this unit is to develop your reading and writing skills through the study of one pair of texts, selected from the six pairs available. Assessment is by a two-part coursework:

- Part A requires you to apply principles of literary and linguistic study to your chosen texts in order to explore the theme specified annually by AQA for each pair of texts (1,200 to 1,500 words).

- Part B requires you to demonstrate your understanding of one or both of your chosen texts by producing a piece of creative writing which extends and enhances the thematic discussion you completed in Part A (500 to 800 words).

Units 1 and 2 comprise the first year or AS part of the course:

Unit 3 (ELLB3): Talk in life and literature
Examination: 2 hours

The emphasis in this unit is on the ways meanings are constructed and conveyed in spoken language. You are required to study one play from a choice of four set plays, which will include at least one by Shakespeare. You will also be required to apply your literary and linguistic understanding to the study of a variety of transcripts of real-life spoken situations. This is a **closed book examination**.

Unit 4 (ELLB4): Text transformation
Coursework

This unit requires you to choose two literary works from a selection of prescribed authors and use them as the basis for the creation of a new

Think about it

Think about how much of your ability in the subject we call English is derived from your experiences in school and how much is derived from ordinary everyday contacts within your network of friends and family.

For example, if you focus on spoken language for the moment, have you considered how you acquired your accent? Have you ever consciously modified the way you speak or been told to by someone else? If so, what does this suggest about the range of attitudes to spoken language?

Key terms

Open book examination: an examination in which you are allowed to take unmarked copies of the books you have studied into the examination room and refer to them if you wish as you write your answers.

Closed book examination: an examination in which you are not allowed to take copies of the books you have studied into the examination room.

text or texts. The new text or texts must be of a different genre from the original and must be between 1,500 and 2,500 words. You also need to write a commentary or commentaries (1,000 to 2,000 words) in which you reflect on the transformation task in order to demonstrate understanding of the creative process.

Units 3 and 4 comprise the second year of the A Level course.

■ Preparation

How should you prepare for approaching your studies in this way? The essential points are that you need to:

■ approach your reading and writing in an integrated way, building on both linguistic and literary understanding and methods
■ develop your creativity and independence as you encounter both spoken and written language
■ think about texts and the relationships between texts, which also requires that you think about the social, cultural and historical contexts of these texts
■ develop independent ways of working so that your individual skills as a producer of spoken and written language are extended, and you also become increasingly thoughtful and responsive in your judgements and evaluations of the language you encounter as reader and as listener.

■ Assessment Objectives

You also need to be clear about the Assessment Objectives (AOs) that underpin all of your studies within this subject. Although the term Assessment Objective may sound a little remote and forbidding, you do need to understand their importance in order to study effectively and give yourself the best possible chance of achieving high grades.

Table 1 *Assessment Objectives for Unit 1*

Assessment Objectives	Questions to ask yourself
AO1 Select and apply relevant concepts and approaches from integrated linguistic and literary study, using appropriate terminology and accurate, coherent written expression	Can I write accurately and coherently about a range of texts of various sorts, using specialist linguistic and literary terms and concepts that will help me to be clear and precise?
AO2 Demonstrate detailed critical understanding in analysing the ways in which structure, form and language shape meanings in a range of spoken and written texts	Can I discuss and write about structure, form and language of spoken and written texts in ways that reveal my critical and analytical understanding?
AO3 Use integrated approaches to explore relationships between texts, analysing the significance of contextual factors in their production and reception	Can I use my linguistic and literary understanding to interpret and evaluate texts and to compare different texts and their social, cultural and historical contexts?
AO4 Demonstrate expertise and creativity in using language appropriately for a variety of purposes and audiences, drawing on insights from literary and linguistic studies	Can I use my linguistic and literary understanding to produce written and spoken language appropriately to communicate effectively with a range of audiences and a range of purposes?

You will have noticed that running through the questions in Table 1 is an insistence on the need to apply your knowledge and understanding of both language and literature, and this is the key to success on this course of study.

How to read

In 2007 John Sutherland, a professor of English, published *How to Read a Novel*, subtitled 'A User's Guide'. This book, which is accessible and well worth reading, raises many issues relevant to your studies at AS and A2 Level in its 28 short chapters. Sutherland shows us the importance of developing autonomy as a reader – that is, approaching our reading thoughtfully and evaluating what we encounter for ourselves, and not uncritically accepting the opinions of others. In his final chapter, for example, Sutherland explains why, for him, Thackeray's *Vanity Fair* is one of the greatest English novels. He also quotes the philosopher Alain de Botton, who describes the book as 'the most overrated ever'. There could hardly be a sharper contrast between their opinions, yet each man is capable of developing a cogent and persuasive case in support of his judgement. You as a reader need to work towards developing your critical and thinking skills so that you can form judgements, advance them and defend them in discussion and writing. It is also important to take your time and hold back from making judgements about texts that you might find unusual or difficult to get to grips with. As far as your examination texts are concerned, you need to persevere especially with works that you find difficult on a first reading, and you need to be receptive to a range of critical and explanatory comment from your teachers, books or web sources. If you eventually judge a book to be flawed in some way and you can establish a clearly argued and well-supported case, you will be demonstrating exactly the kinds of skills and understanding that will entitle you to high marks in the examinations or in your coursework. Look again at AO3 and the corresponding third question in Table 1.

Before you begin to think in detail about how to read a novel (or a play, poem or non-fiction text), you need to ask an even more fundamental question: Why am I reading this book? More specifically, what exactly is my purpose as a reader? At different times in your reading lives you will doubtless have a wide range of justifications or reasons for reading. Because you are following a course in English Language and Literature, it is a safe bet that you enjoy reading as a leisure activity and you value the contacts you have via the printed page with the thoughts, ideas, stories and experiences of others.

Of the myriad possible answers to the question 'Why am I reading this book?', perhaps the most likely is that you derive some kind of pleasure or satisfaction from doing so. However, for the reading you do as part of the English Language and Literature course, you will almost certainly have an additional reason, a pragmatic or utilitarian one; to achieve the highest possible grades as a passport to a university place or a career.

Different kinds of reading can fit into three main categories:

- *Reading the lines:* reading for surface meanings. Much of our day-to-day reading takes place at this level: skimming a newspaper for details of what is on television, checking how long the ready meal needs in the microwave or reading a gossip column in a magazine, for example.

Think about it

Think about the different types of reading in relation to the following quotations about how we read and what the effects of reading can be.

'Some books are to be tasted, others to be swallowed, and some few are to be chewed and digested.'
Francis Bacon (1561–1626)

'A conventional good read is usually a bad read, a relaxing bath in what we know already. A true good read is surely an act of innovative creation in which we, the readers, become conspirators.'
Malcolm Bradbury (1932–2000)

'Reading a book is like re-writing it for yourself … You bring to a novel, anything you read, all your experience of the world. You bring your history and you read it in your own terms.'
Angela Carter (1940–92)

'There is creative reading as well as creative writing.'
Ralph Waldo Emerson (1803–82)

'Books give not wisdom where none was before. But where some is, there reading makes it more.'
John Harington (1561–1612)

'What is reading, but silent conversation.'
Walter Savage Landor (1775–1864)

▓ *Reading between the lines:* this requires the reader to be alert to what a text hints at or implies, as well as what is stated explicitly. This is the kind of careful 'reading in low gear' that you must engage in as you study your examination texts; they have been selected for study because they offer richness and complexity of various sorts. They are not so much puzzles to be solved as creations of the writers' imaginations and they offer language and ideas which you, as a reader, need to interpret and enjoy on a number of levels, including the intellectual and the imaginative. You cannot study them adequately if you simply skim-read them and students who do not apply their skills of inference, evaluation and judgement will not be working in the ways necessary for success at AS, let alone A2, level.

▓ *Reading beyond the lines:* this refers to the ability of readers to extend their thinking so that their understanding of a particular book is related to their experience of life, their knowledge of other books, their attitudes to moral issues, their judgements about artistic values – indeed, the whole of a reader's awareness of his or her world. Some books can affect us so much that we are forced to take stock of what we really believe and what we really feel; reading beyond the lines enables us to develop as individuals. We engage so closely with a book that we allow it to expand our awareness, our understanding, our values: it can help to make us, in some small way, different people after we have read the book from the people we were before.

▓ Developing your skills

How can you best develop the skills and understanding necessary for success in your English Language and Literature B course? The obvious answer to that question is, of course, to study your set texts and language topics carefully, but that on its own is not enough. You also need to develop your ability to talk and write about books effectively, and that takes practice and a willingness to learn from others.

An excellent starting point is to listen to or watch radio or television programmes about books and reading. Here are some suggestions of programmes that will widen your knowledge:

▓ *Bookclub* (Radio 4) brings a small panel of readers face to face with a writer to discuss one of his or her books. It is available on the BBC Radio website using the 'Listen Again' feature and gives an excellent insight into different readers' responses to the novel and the writer's approaches to writing.

▓ *A Good Read* (Radio 4) involves discussion between three readers of a chosen book. Sometimes they agree about the merits of a particular book, but often they disagree. Listening to a discussion in which three intelligent readers express different views about the same book conveys a powerful message: what matters most is your personal response to books and your ability to explain and, where necessary, defend your position.

▓ *World Book Club* and *The Word* on the BBC Radio World Service – programmes can be listened to again via the website.

▓ *Emagazine* is a subscription magazine and website aimed specifically at all English A Level students with articles on a wide variety of authors and topics.

■ Try reading book reviews in the Saturday editions of newspapers such as the *Guardian*, the *Independent*, the *Times* and the *Daily Telegraph* and their Sunday editions. These reviews will help to familiarise you with the process of evaluating and conveying to others your judgements and responses to your reading.

Remember, though, that the AS and A2 course is designed to develop your personal responses, and not to turn you into an obedient mouthpiece for the views of this critic or that critic. If you enter the examination room having acquired detailed knowledge of your set texts and topics, as well as independent judgement, you are well prepared for success in the exam and the benefits that come from a lifetime's experience of being a good reader and a thoughtful writer.

This unit covers:

■ exploring the relationships between texts, using integrated critical approaches to language and literature

■ demonstrating detailed critical understanding, using appropriate terminology

■ demonstrating expertise and creativity in using language appropriately for a variety of purposes.

AQA Examiner's tip

Read both of your set books straight through as early in the course as you can. Then when you come to study them in detail you will see more easily the coursework opportunities that are open to you.

■ Introduction

The AS coursework in English Language and Literature B is designed to help you do two things:

■ to deepen your knowledge and understanding of books by other writers

■ to show this understanding through creative work of your own.

The two are closely connected. As you read and comment on other people's writing, you will gain ideas that you can put into practice when you are the author yourself.

Your tasks

In this coursework unit, Themes in language and literature, you will be studying two full-length texts, written at different periods but with some connection between them. This connection might be genre-based (for example, detective stories), the same topic (for example, survival) or the same audience (for example, children). One of the books might be a sequel or prequel to the other, or an adaptation of its ideas.

Chapters 1–10 of this book discuss a range of ideas and approaches to help you consider how meanings are constructed and how you as a reader can engage with the meanings of these and other texts. In Chapter 11 there is a worked example to show how you might tackle the first part of the coursework. You can then build on this knowledge in Chapters 12–14, which give suggestions for the kind of creative writing you might produce yourself, with complete examples in Chapter 15.

Your candidate brief

Unit 2 is assessed through two coursework tasks – there is no examination. As you begin to study the texts you will be given a prescribed theme to consider, and both tasks will be related to this.

You are going to study in detail what each author has to say and the way in which he or she says it. You will then show your understanding as follows:

■ Part A of the coursework you produce will analyse the way a particular theme appears in two short extracts from the set texts. You choose these extracts yourself. The analysis should then be 1200–1500 words long. This assignment carries 40 out of 64 marks.

■ Part B will show your understanding of the texts by asking you to adapt your set texts creatively in some way. This should be 500–850 words long. It carries 24 out of 64 marks.

The complete coursework unit carries 40 per cent of the marks for AS English Language and Literature.

You are not required to submit drafts or commentaries for assessment, but you will need to show evidence of planning. This should be a handwritten document and should deal with both tasks. You can do so in a single task covering both texts, or two separate tasks covering each task individually.

In this paper, your work will be assessed according to the relevant Assessment Objectives. Think of these as questions the examiner will be asking you.

AO1 tests your ability to select and apply relevant concepts and approaches from integrated linguistic and literary study.	This means that you will need to understand how best to approach the study of each text, selecting from a range of possible approaches.
AO2 tests your ability to demonstrate detailed critical understanding in analysing the ways in which structure, form and language shape meanings in a range of spoken and written texts.	This means that you will need to analyse language, commenting on how choices of words and phrases, as well as the use of particular kinds of sentence patterns, influence the effects that writers and speakers have on readers and listeners.
AO3 tests your ability to use integrated approaches to explore relationships between texts, analysing and evaluating the significance of contextual factors in their production and reception.	This means that you will need to compare different texts, showing how they might be similar and how they might be different in the ways they convey meaning and influence the attitudes, feelings and actions of readers and listeners. The second part of AO3 focuses on 'contextual factors', which means that you will be expected to comment on the circumstances in which texts are spoken or written and heard or read.
AO4 demonstrate expertise and creativity in using language appropriately for a variety of purposes and audiences drawing on insights from literary and linguistic studies.	Can I use my linguistic and literary understanding to produce written and spoken language appropriately to communicate effectively with a range of audiences and for a range of purposes?

This unit discusses as wide a range of texts and ideas as possible. We shall also be referring to two specific themes and pairings of texts as worked examples in Chapters 11 and 15. These are:

■ Suspense – in *The Woman in White* and *The Lady in the Lake*
■ Social class – in *North and South* and *The Road to Wigan Pier*.

Practical activity

As you work through the set texts, keep a part of your file where you can note a range of ideas for creative writing. These might be points where the set text could be expanded with new material, ideas for seeing plot developments from a different point of view, or notes on characters. Keep firmly focused on your set theme while you do this.

Write down the number of the page in the text that gave you these ideas, so that you can come back to it later.

Working with your set texts

Two set texts

The point of studying two texts that are related thematically is that by comparing them you get a greater insight into what each author is doing. Comparing the similarities helps you to notice the differences too. For example, *Heart of Darkness* and *Blood River* are both accounts of a journey of discovery which takes place on the River Congo. Both are first person accounts and make use of the writer's own experiences. However, the worlds in which Joseph Conrad and Tim Butcher live are very different.

Practical activity

Think about these two brief extracts. In each of them the speaker makes plans for his expedition. You will be able to guess fairly easily which is Conrad's narrative dating from 1899 and which is Butcher's of 2006.

You might look at:

- the attitudes to empire
- the mention of technology
- the levels of formality in the language.

1 We exchanged emails. Brian jokingly dismissed his motorbike adventure as an 'interesting way to get a sore backside' and I eventually summoned the courage to ask him directly if I could borrow a motorbike and a guide from his Care International staff. The fact that he did not turn me down flat meant I was in with a chance.

2 In a very few hours I arrived in a city that always makes me think of a whited sepulchre. Prejudice no doubt. I had no difficulty in finding the Company's offices. It was the biggest thing in town, and everybody I met was full of it. They were going to run an over-sea empire, and make no end of coin by trade.

Finding links between texts

The pair of texts you will study are linked in some way by their subject matter, but in each case the two are separated from one another by a gap of at least 50 years in their dates of publication. This means that they will have considerable differences. For example, there may be differences that relate to their social and historical contexts, as well as differences of language and style that are characteristic of the periods in which the texts were written. To bring out the significance of each text, first of all you need to be able to distinguish between what happens in the **narrative** and the writer's technique in ordering and describing events. You also need some appropriate critical vocabulary to help you do this.

Key terms

Narrative: an account of connected events.

Although every text is different, each writer shares common problems of how to shape the narrative and keep the reader's attention. All texts here use speech; they all introduce and develop characters; they all place the action in particular settings, even though the ways that writers present matters differ greatly. Comparing the ways in which different authors shape their material helps you to appreciate the individual qualities of each narrative.

As you study the different topics, you will find examples from books other than the ones your own coursework will be based on. This will widen your general background in literary criticism, and help you to grasp some of the broader concepts of analysis. What you learn about techniques of writing can be applied to any literary prose, and will help you to become a better writer yourself.

Approaching analysis

You have already learned a good deal about critical approaches in Unit 1 and you need to be able to apply that knowledge here. However, so far you will have studied short extracts or poems rather than full-length prose works. There are a few new critical terms for you to learn as you explore longer narratives.

This section is divided up into different topics for convenience, but in the end it is never entirely possible to separate what writers say from the way they say it. Matters such as character description, speech and sentence length all contribute in different proportions to the overall meaning, and they all shade into one another. You might think of it as like a kaleidoscope, each little bit contributing to a larger pattern.

A word of warning here – your work needs to focus on the actual written texts. Many novels and biographies have been adapted to make films. Some of these are excellent, and you might even consider writing part of a film script yourself for the second part of your coursework, but they are always different in some way from the original text. Remember, it is the original texts you are studying and writing about in your coursework.

AQA Examiner's tip

The sections that follow identify features of writing that you may need to comment on in critical analysis, and definitions of technical terms. What the examiner is looking for is not simply the ability to spot and name any of these features, but that you can use these terms to analyse how the authors create meaning in texts.

■ Think about it

Compare these short snatches of dialogue in different styles and decide whether they have the same effect. Which is more polite? Which is more forceful? Would they provoke the same reaction from the listener?

- 'Would you mind moving, please?'
- 'Clear off!'

■ Practical activity

If you have access to a film version of your set book, make a list of the differences between the two and consider why the alterations have been made. Among other things, this activity often gives an insight into changes over time, including aspects such as audience expectations, language style and narrative techniques.

Answers:
Writer 1 is Butcher
Writer 2 is Conrad

2   What do we mean by themes in language and literature?

Key terms

Plot: the arrangement of narrative events in a story organised in such a way as to create links between them and maintain interest for the reader.

Episodic: an episodic narrative consists of a series of events that do not overlap or affect each other – for example, the main character moves from place to place, having different adventures in each.

Episode: a self-contained event that can be identified within the main sequence of events in the narrative.

Picaresque: a novel that describes the adventures, usually comic, of a lively and resourceful hero on a journey. The name comes from the Spanish word *pícaro*, which means rascal.

Narrative structures: the storyline and its development

Plot and theme

For each year in which particular text pairings are set, AQA will set the themes to be used as the focus for coursework analysis and creative writing tasks. So what *are* themes?

Themes are ideas that emerge and recur as the narrative progresses. They are aspects of the writer's treatment of material that make the text distinctively different from others, because the ideas in a book are more complicated than just the basic sequence of events. To understand how this works, we need to go back a little and talk first about story and **plot**. It is the plot structure that allows the themes to develop within it.

When we start to read or tell stories, the first thing we notice is what happens, the simple sequence of events. At first children write 'and then ... and then ... and then ...' when they start to make up stories, just using the simple order of time. Mature writers soon begin to see that it is the pattern of events that matters, so the story will evolve into a more complex plot. Various themes develop as this plot unfolds.

Consider this story: a poor woman meets a rich and desirable man. He falls for her, they are separated by difficulties, but are eventually reunited and enabled to marry. Do you recognise this plot in any of the texts you have read? It is a common one in fiction.

This is the story of *Cinderella*, of course, but it is also the basic storyline of *North and South*, with Mr Bell, the old Oxford don, in the role of the fairy godfather. The two texts are very different in effect. They may have the same underlying story structure, but they are distinct in time, place and ways of telling. *North and South* carries contrasting themes from the old fairy tale, such as industrial development and social conflict.

Sometimes a framework plot contains a number of little stories within it that are linked in some way. Mark Twain makes a joke about the **episodic** structure of his novel *The Adventures of Huckleberry Finn*, saying that 'persons attempting to find a plot in it will be shot', but he knows very well that this kind of narrative, with adventures linked by a journey, is another typical plot pattern. It has a long literary history, going back as far as the sixteenth century. Its characteristic themes include the resourcefulness and courage of the low-life hero, like Huck. Some of the earliest novels ever written use this structure, and there is even a technical name for it – the **picaresque**.

Practical activity

Try reducing the storyline of each of the two books you are studying to no more than three sentences. If you can see how the skeleton of the story works, it might help you find material for creative work based on it.

Writers shape their narrative structures carefully; even some non-fiction, which at first sight seems to be organised by time sequence, shows this. So, in *Alive* Piers Paul Read structures his chapters to switch from the survivors of the air crash to the various attempts to look for them, keeping different strands of the narrative going at the same time. George Orwell's persuasive series of essays, *The Road to Wigan Pier*, moves by degrees from description of life in the north of England to a discussion of socialism.

E. M. Forster discusses the idea of sequence in *Aspects of the Novel*, where he explains it very memorably. He says that 'The king died and then the queen died' is a story, but 'The king died, and then the queen died of grief' is a plot – one event depends on the other and themes emerge during this process.

Plot is important; it keeps us turning the pages. When you come to choose your extracts for analysis, you might focus on a moment of discovery or an important event. But although you might notice how your chosen extract contributes to the plot, this is subtly different from theme. Theme provides an extra connection between events.

In the example of the king and queen there might be two themes. One is death, because this obviously happens more than once, so is a recurring idea in this narrative. The other possible theme is grief, which is not an event at all, but an emotion. You can imagine other possible plots and themes arising from the same story. Perhaps the queen murdered the king and then took her own life in a fit of guilt. If we investigated the queen's reactions this might give us another theme – guilt.

Themes are unifying ideas that the writer explores and develops in the course of a narrative.

Plot structures

The classic plot structure goes like this:

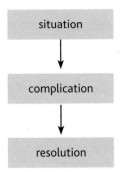

In the beginning, the author has to set time and place, introduce the main characters and establish a point of view. He or she has to make us want to read on. At the end, the author has to resolve the issues in some way satisfactory to the reader or else, as Raymond Chandler once said, the story is 'an unresolved chord, and leaves irritation behind it.'

Beginnings

Openings are extremely important in attracting the reader's attention. What information do you normally expect at the beginning of a narrative?

■ Further reading

■ E. M. Forster, *Aspects of the Novel*, Penguin Classics, 2005

■ **Key terms**

Themes: major subjects in a text, often representing ideas that recur during the narrative.

■ Practical activity

Make a list of the kinds of information you expected to find in the opening of the texts you are studying. Compare your list of expected information with what the writer actually provides. Do you find any surprises?

Robinson Crusoe tells us about his family and early life, but *The Catcher in the Rye* begins with Holden Caulfield positively refusing to give information about his background. He refers contemptuously to the material Dickens uses in the opening of *David Copperfield* and complains that it bores him.

If you look carefully at the first paragraph of J. D. Salinger's novel you will see that the main stress falls on the personality and language of Holden Caulfield. Salinger establishes Holden's characteristic uneasiness, his habit of exaggeration and his slangy, colloquial speech patterns.

J. D. Salinger is deliberately withholding information in order to make us read on. We do want to know about the background of the person who is speaking to us, but we are going to have to wait a little and work it out for ourselves. In the meantime, stress falls on the personality and language of Holden Caulfield, establishing his characteristic uneasiness, his habit of exaggeration and his use of colloquial language.

Largely because his narrative is non-fiction, Tim Butcher has to convey a lot of necessary background in *Blood River* concerning the nature of his projected journey down the River Congo and his motivation for undertaking it. Instead of making us wait until the third chapter for the expedition to get going, he begins with a preface describing his sensations at one particular point of the journey, when he paused in the town of Kalemie, waiting for transport. 'Outside was the Congo,' he says, 'and I was terrified.' Many writers use this kind of technique, beginning some way into the story, then going back to fill in necessary information later.

 ### Critical response activity

Here is the opening paragraph of George Orwell's *The Road to Wigan Pier*. What information does this brief extract give you about the book's setting?

> The first sound in the mornings was the clumping of the mill-girls' clogs down the cobbled street. Earlier than that, I suppose, there were factory whistles which I was never awake to hear.

Commentary

This establishes a location because of the mention of mills and factories. It does this through an appeal to the sense of hearing, the sound of the clogs on cobbles and the factory whistles. It also explains that Orwell himself is an outsider and observer here. He knows that the whistles blow, but can ignore them and sleep on. Later, he will explain why he is in the industrial north of England. For the moment, we are simply plunged into an unfamiliar scene.

All these narratives have openings that are both economical and striking, rapidly conveying information and setting the tone, ensuring that they engage our interest quickly. Each of these writers also begins to establish themes. Salinger introduces Holden's rejection of authority; Butcher shows us his powerful sense of danger; and we become involved with Orwell in the working life of the north of England.

Novice writers may find this hard to do, often beginning too far back with something a little dull, when they would be better off starting further into the story, then revealing more of the background later. Openings are especially important, and worth some extra attention as you plan, compose and revise your own writing.

AQA Examiner's tip

This is something you might bear in mind for your coursework. A striking opening creates momentum in a story. You might well write the opening last, or return to your first attempt and redraft it in light of the way your narrative has developed.

Endings

How does a writer resolve the complications of his or her narrative? The main endings of many texts are natural and obvious; a travel book such as *Blood River* will naturally finish with the end of the journey. J. G. Ballard's *Empire of the Sun* ends with Jim reunited with his parents at the end of the war.

One of the most frequent endings in fiction is marriage. *The Woman in White* ends with Laura Fairlie safely married to Walter Hartright, with their child heir to a fortune, while although in *North and South* Margaret Hale and Mr Thornton are not actually married, Elizabeth Gaskell implies that they soon will be. Vera Brittain's non-fiction autobiography *Testament of Youth* also ends at a conventional point as she prepares to marry.

Heart of Darkness, which begins with a splendidly cinematic opening of a sunset over the Thames, returns to the same location at the end of the narrative to round it off, and in order to stress the universal nature of evil.

> The offing was barred by a black bank of clouds, and the tranquil waterway leading to the uttermost ends of the earth flowed sombre under an overcast sky – seemed to lead into the heart of an immense darkness.

Writers often feel an obligation to tie up the loose ends. *Robinson Crusoe* and *Alive* both take the narrative a little beyond the actual rescue.

■ Critical response activity

The main complications in the story are resolved at the ending of *The Adventures of Huckleberry Finn*. Huck Finn's adventures are neatly rounded off when he is reunited with Tom Sawyer and when the long-suffering Jim is finally released.

However, here are his actual last words. Can you see any possibility beyond the general rounding-off?

> If I'd a knowed what trouble it was to make a book I wouldn't a tackled it and ain't a-going to no more. But I reckon I got to light out for the Territory ahead of the rest, because Aunt Sally she's going to adopt me and sivilize me and I can't stand it. I been there before.

That word 'But' is significant: there is an obvious opening for a sequel. Mark Twain never did expand on Huck's adventures, but he leaves himself the opportunity to describe what happens in the future when Aunt Sally does actually try to 'sivilize' him. Daniel Defoe, though, did write a sequel to *Robinson Crusoe* – *The Farther Adventures of Robinson Crusoe*.

This is something you might consider in planning your creative writing coursework. Did Holden Caulfield really go back to school and make a success of it? Did Margaret Hale actually marry John Thornton and live happily ever after?

Genre

Genre is not the same as theme or structure, but the three are often related. Often we expect a narrative to follow a particular pattern before we ever start reading it. We may have previous experience of the same kind of writing.

■ Key terms

Genre: a class or category of text with its particular conventions of language, form and structure – for example, short story, science-fiction novel, Shakespearean comedy.

The idea of genre is one way of recognising similarities between the structures and subject matter of different texts, and so grouping them. It means the special kind of writing a text belongs to, and this is important because the reader will have different expectations from different narrative forms.

The term genre is used in one way to denote very broad classes of writing. The broadest and most obvious genres in literature are defined by the forms of language, being prose, poetry and plays. That is only the beginning, however. Within the genre of literary prose, which is what we are discussing in this unit, you will be aware of narrower classifications:

- novels
- short stories
- biography
- travel writing.

Some of these categories are fiction, others based on fact, and it is not necessarily easy to find the dividing line between the two. Often novels reflect the writer's personal experience, as is the case with J. G. Ballard's *Empire of the Sun*. Vera Brittain tells us how she considered presenting her material in different formats, both fiction and non-fiction, before deciding to write her **autobiography**.

> My original idea was that of a long novel, and I started to plan it. To my dismay it turned out a hopeless failure; I never got much further than the planning, for I found that the people and events about which I was writing were still too near and too real to be made the subjects of an imaginative, detached reconstruction.
>
> Then I tried the effect of reproducing parts of the long diary which I kept from 1913 to 1918, with fictitious names substituted for all the real ones out of consideration for the many persons still alive who were mentioned in it with a youthful and sometimes rather cruel candour. This too was a failure. Apart from the fact that the diary ended too soon to give a complete picture, the fictitious names created a false atmosphere and made the whole thing seem spurious.
>
> There was only one possible course left – to tell my own fairly typical story as truthfully as I could against the larger background, and take the risk of offending all those who believe that a personal story should be kept private.

The genre of the novel itself can include a wide range of styles and subject matter. We expect it to be long – several hours of reading time – and to have a large number of characters (whereas the short story will be more strictly limited in both these ways), but this still leaves almost infinite possibilities for variation. Within this general genre of novels there will be subgenres with different characteristics, and it is at this level that genre is most likely to relate to either setting or theme. Some examples might be:

- realist novels
- science fiction
- detective stories
- Gothic horror
- historical novels.

Some genres may be written for particular audiences. Romances on the whole are read by a female audience; war stories on the whole by a male one, though *Testament of Youth* may be an exception. Some genres may have particular settings and subject matter. For example, science fiction often takes us out into space.

Some genres have widely recognised rules of structure; the detective story is one of them. Raymond Chandler listed 'ten commandments for the detective novel' and it is very interesting to relate them to *The Lady in the Lake*. They are:

1 It must be credibly motivated, both as to the original situation and the denouement.

2 It must be technically sound as to the methods of murder and detection.

3 It must be realistic in character, setting, and atmosphere. It must be about real people in a real world.

4 It must have a sound story value apart from the mystery element; i.e. the investigation itself must be an adventure worth reading.

5 It must have enough essential simplicity to be explained easily when the time comes.

6 It must baffle a reasonably intelligent reader.

7 The solution must seem inevitable once revealed.

8 It must not try to do everything at once. If it is a puzzle story operating in a rather cool, reasonable atmosphere, it cannot also be a violent adventure or passionate romance.

9 It must punish the criminal in one way or another, not necessarily by operation of the law … if the detective fails to resolve the consequences of the crime, the story is an unresolved chord and leaves irritation behind it.

10 It must be honest with the reader.

Quoted in N. Parsons, The Book of Literary Lists, *1986*

The mystery must be resolved; the crime must be punished. This list is unusually detailed, but Chandler is not simply writing to a formula here. He is saying that readers will have expectations of the genre before they pick up the book, and that structure, as well as setting and characterisation, must take account of these expectations.

The influence of methods of publication

The method of publication has contributed to the structure of some of the set texts. Both *North and South* and *The Woman in White* were originally published as instalments in Charles Dickens's weekly periodicals *Household Words* and *All the Year Round* respectively. You can see this in the structure of both novels. The chapters are short and many of them have endings that create suspense. The writer has to keep the story moving week by week; consequently he or she leaves situations unresolved and maintains themes for as long as possible.

Think about it

New methods of publication and new genres arise all the time – for example, the blog is a modern means of communication. How could you make creative use of this?

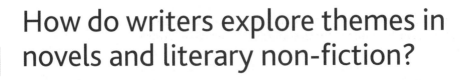

3 How do writers explore themes in novels and literary non-fiction?

Point of view: who tells the story?

Each narrative has a characteristic voice. The way the story is told will colour its whole meaning. There is an important difference between a narrator who is part of the action and one who is an outside observer of it. Both methods have their advantages and limitations.

There is a difference, too, between a narrator telling what happens through description and comment and showing it through action or dialogue (which we shall consider later).

First-person narrative

This is the way of telling a story that uses the pronoun 'I'. It is the most common method in the selection of texts that AQA has chosen, both for fiction and non-fiction. The first-person narrative is, of course, the most intimate. We hear the voice of the character directly, sharing his or her experience. Often the reader identifies with the speaker's point of view as the narrative progresses.

Critical response activity

Take this moment from *The Lady in the Lake*, where a corrupt policeman chases the detective through derelict and lonely streets. What are the advantages and disadvantages of having Philip Marlowe tell the story himself?

> The car came up level and started to cut in. I stood the Chrysler on its nose, swung out behind the police car, and made a U turn with half an inch to spare. I gunned the motor the other way. Behind me sounded the rough clashing of gears, the howl of an infuriated motor, and the red spotlight swept for what seemed miles over the brickyard.
>
> It wasn't any use. They were behind me and coming fast again. I didn't have any idea of getting away. I wanted to get back where there were houses and people to come out and watch and perhaps to remember.
>
> I didn't make it.

Commentary

One advantage of the first-person narrative in this case is that it generates excitement. The suspense is tremendous as we follow the narrator move by move. Short phrases quicken the pace, generating a sense of urgency. As his enemy closes in, and Marlowe reacts to imminent danger, we sympathise with him. He can give us close detail about how he 'made a U turn with half an inch to spare'; he can describe sense impressions, such as the sounds of 'the rough clashing of gears, the howl of an infuriated motor'; and he can emphasise his own thoughts and sensations.

The chief disadvantage is that the hero has to stay alive to tell the story, unless the writer can find some exceptionally clever way of solving this problem. Marlowe may be beaten up, but somehow he has to be rescued.

A first-person narrative gives opportunities for powerful impressions. The reader will tend to identify closely with the action, but there will always be some limitation. We can see events only as the **protagonist** sees them. Inevitably the point of view will be biased. However, writers can use this bias creatively and to their advantage.

One way of taking advantage of our close insight into the events of a first-person narrative is by using multiple narrators and making the reader compare them. *The Woman in White* has no fewer than ten different first-person narrators, although some of them have very small parts in the plot.

Key terms

Protagonist: the leading character, or one of the main characters, in a literary text.

Critical response activity

How does Wilkie Collins influence our reactions to this narrator's voice in *The Woman in White?*

The speaker is the hero, Walter Hartright. He is a poor drawing master and has just fallen in love with his rich and beautiful pupil, Laura Fairlie.

> I should have remembered my position, and have put myself secretly on my guard. I did so, but not until it was too late. All the discretion, all the experience, which had availed me with other women, and secured me against other temptations, failed me with her. It had been my profession, for years past, to be in this close contact with young girls of all ages, and of all orders of beauty. I had accepted the position as part of my calling in life; I had trained myself to leave all the sympathies natural to my age in my employer's outer hall, as coolly as I left my umbrella there before I went upstairs. I had long since learned to understand, composedly and as a matter of course, that my situation in life was considered a guarantee against any of my female pupils feeling more than the most ordinary interest in me, and that I was admitted among beautiful and captivating women much as a harmless domestic animal is admitted among them.

Commentary

The theme here is Hartright's sincere but apparently hopeless love. Collins portrays him as an honest man, regretful because he 'should have remembered' his social position, but blaming no one but himself for his difficulties. He is clear and open in describing his status as a paid employee and in analysing his feelings in detail. The long sentences, with their subordinate clauses, give a reflective feel to the passage. Hartright has a realistic and objective view of his relationship with his pupils because of his experience of 'years past'. At the same time, the reminder that he is a handsome and active young man with what he calls 'all the sympathies natural to my age', and the rueful comparison with 'a harmless domestic animal', both make us feel sorry for him. His only fault is that he is poor.

Usually, though not always, we can assume that first-person narrators are telling the truth as they see it, but this does not mean that the reader necessarily has to accept everything they say. For various reasons, a narrator may be unreliable.

Critical response activity

Now compare Hartright's tone with the effect of a different first-person narrative within *The Woman in White*.

> It is the grand misfortune of my life that nobody will let me alone.
>
> Why – I ask everybody – why worry me? Nobody answers that question, and nobody lets me alone. Relatives, friends and strangers all combine to annoy me. What have I done? I ask myself, I ask my servant Louis, fifty times a day – what have I done? Neither of us can tell. Most extraordinary!

Commentary

The speaker here is Frederick Fairlie, whom one of the other characters describes as 'a maudlin, twaddling, selfish fool'. Fairlie is mainly concerned to avoid any trouble to himself. We see this emphasised in the repetition of 'let me alone' and 'what have I done?' The broken rhythms of the speech express peevish irritation. Collins does not expect us to share Fairlie's point of view; in fact he is an obstacle in the plot because he refuses his help to the main characters. We make an **ironic** judgement on his character.

Collins fits the different first-person accounts together like pieces in a jigsaw, contrasting speakers and making us judge them. He reveals each character through his or her own words, and we might, as readers, understand more about the narrators than they do about themselves.

Using different formats

Another way of solving the problems of having a limited viewpoint is to bring in something like a letter or a diary. A letter can give information that the character reading it would not otherwise have known and add another voice to the narrative.

Modern narratives often include documents of various kinds, as a way of emphasising their authenticity. For example, Tim Butcher illustrates different points in *Blood River* with a copy of the laissez-passer issued to him by the authorities in Katanga and an extract from Katharine Hepburn's diary, written while she was on location filming *The African Queen*. George Orwell includes details of miners' pay-cheques in *The Road to Wigan Pier*.

In *Testament of Youth* Vera Brittain uses a variety of poems, mostly written by herself or her fiancé Roland Leighton, to vary the text and deepen its emotional impact.

Third-person narrative

The omniscient author

In the style of writing that uses the pronouns 'he', 'she', 'they', the narrator may be the author, or may be a different character. One of the advantages of this method of telling a story is that the author can see everything that is going on, including what goes on in the minds of different characters, and can describe scenes where he or she was not present. This form of narrative is conveyed by an **omniscient narrator** (that is, one who is all-seeing and all-knowing). It was very popular in nineteenth-century novels, but tends to be less used today.

Key terms

Irony: a mismatch or discrepancy between what is written and what is actually meant – for example, where the reader makes a judgement of the narrator by using a different set of values or taking a different point of view.

Think about it

Letters are a way of expanding the information in a text by giving a different viewpoint. You might consider a letter from one of the characters in the narrative you are studying as a way of presenting your creative writing coursework.

Key terms

Omniscient narrator: a third-person point of view that allows an 'all-knowing' author to describe both outward details and a character's inner thoughts and feelings. Omniscient narrators can move freely between different characters and scenes, with full knowledge of everything that happens. They are able to comment on events and themes as well as describing them.

Critical response activity

■ How does Elizabeth Gaskell develop the character of Margaret in the extract from *North and South* below?

■ What effect does the author's own voice have on the narrative?

> Margaret went out heavily and unwillingly enough. But the length of a street – yes, the air of a Milton street – cheered her young blood before she reached her first turning. Her step grew lighter, her lip redder. She began to take notice, instead of having her thoughts turned exclusively inward. She saw unusual loiterers in the streets: men with their hands in their pockets sauntering along; loud-laughing and loud-spoken girls clustered together, apparently excited to high spirits, and a boisterous independence of temper and behaviour. The more ill-looking of the men – the discreditable minority – hung about on the steps of the beer-houses and gin shops, smoking and commenting pretty freely on every passer-by. Margaret disliked the prospect of the long walk through these streets, before she came to the fields which she had planned to reach. Instead she would go and see Bessy Higgins. It would not be so refreshing as a quiet country walk, but still it would perhaps be doing the kinder thing.

Commentary

Gaskell is able to tell us not only what Margaret does as she sets out for her walk, but also what she is thinking and feeling. She went out 'unwillingly', but soon 'began to take notice'. She 'disliked' the prospect of passing through noisy streets and so changed her plans. Although this is a third-person narrative, shown from the outside, there is a suggestion of Margaret's own characteristic style of language in the sentence: 'It would not be so refreshing as a quiet country walk, but still it would perhaps be doing the kinder thing.' In addition, Gaskell adds some of her own opinions and comments. In the phrase 'yes, the air of a Milton street', she is referring to the way some of her characters have compared the northern town unfavourably with the country and thus disagreeing with them. The defence of Milton as a vigorous and enterprising place is a major theme in the novel.

In the descriptive detail of the 'loud-spoken' girls, or 'ill-looking' and 'discreditable' men in the streets, Gaskell is preparing us for the theme of industrial conflict in a later scene, when a strike becomes violent and Margaret is caught in the middle of it.

This kind of narrative is flexible and gives the writer opportunities to range widely over time, space and ideas. One possible disadvantage, however, is that the author's voice may become too intrusive and modern writers will often try to avoid this.

Empire of the Sun is also a third-person narrative, where J. G. Ballard knows what his hero Jim is thinking and feeling, but he takes care to make his own voice less obvious, leaving it to the reader to make judgements or supply missing information. At one point in the story, Jim, aged ten, is forced to drink from the polluted River Yangtze. Ballard gives a dead-pan description of the scene.

> The brown water swelled glassily round the pier, and he remembered that his father had told him how sunlight killed bacteria. Fifty yards away the corpse of a young Chinese woman floated among the sampans, heels rotating around her head as if unsure in what direction to point her that day. Cautiously, Jim decanted a little water from one palm to the other, then drank quickly so that the germs would have no time to infect him.

The point of view here is complex. The narrator's voice describing events in the third person is presumably that of the author, but is actually the point of view of the child. Educated adult readers will see the danger that the child does not, because they know perfectly well that sunlight does not make water safe when there are corpses floating in it, and that swallowing quickly will have no effect whatsoever on the 'germs'. The gap between the readers' perception and the child's ignorance makes the scene all the more horrific.

Critical response activity

In this later scene from *Empire of the Sun*, Dr Ransome, Jim and a number of other prisoners, desperately ill and near death, are driven from prison camp to prison camp, waiting to be taken in and interned by the Japanese.

How does Ballard use irony here?

> For ten minutes the Japanese soldiers argued with one another, while the driver waited with Dr Ransome. Two senior British prisoners stepped through the gates and joined the discussion.
>
> 'Woosung camp?'
>
> 'No, no, no ...'
>
> 'Who sent them? In this condition?'
>
> Avoiding Dr Ransome, they approached the truck and stared at the prisoners through the cloud of flies. As Jim kicked his heels and whistled to himself they watched him without expression. The Japanese sentries opened the barbed-wire gates, but the British prisoners immediately closed them and began to shout at the Japanese sergeant. When Dr Ransome stepped forward to remonstrate with them the British waved him away.
>
> 'Get back, man ...'
>
> 'We can't take you, doctor. There are children here.'

Commentary

Ballard makes no overt comment on what happens in this scene (although the chapter does end with Jim's feeling of rejection), but the point is clear. As happens a number of times in this novel, the British behave worse than the Japanese. The irony is that their excuse for turning away prisoners, 'There are children here,' is used against a British child. Attentive readers will observe this and make their own judgements without further comment from the narrator, who is kept in the background.

4 Narrative structures: 'showing' and 'telling'

The difference between 'showing' and 'telling'

Sometimes writers want to cover ground as quickly as possible by 'telling' the reader what happens. Sometimes, though, it is more important to enable us to visualise the scene, so a situation like 'He waited impatiently in the office' might be shown more strongly as 'He paced up and down the office floor, glaring fixedly at the clerk who was ignoring him.' Carefully selected detail is one way of 'showing' rather than 'telling'.

Including direct speech to make the action more dramatic is another very important method of 'showing' events.

This chapter covers:

■ bringing narrative to life

■ the importance of dialogue in narrative structure

■ recognising the uses of dialect.

Critical response activity

Look at this paragraph from *Blood River*, where Tim Butcher is making part of his journey down the Congo overland, riding pillion over rough tracks on a motorbike belonging to one of the aid agencies in the region.

Which part of his narrative is 'telling' and which part is 'showing'?

> The rest of that day was pure purgatory. My backside had stopped being numb and had moved into a painful phase, each buttock screaming to be relieved of the pressure of being squashed against the plastic of Odimba's motorbike seat. I learned to lean on one side and then the other to alleviate the pressure, but it was agony.

Commentary

The first sentence here is a comment from the writer, summarising or 'telling' his feelings. He then backs this up with graphic detail, 'showing' exactly how he was suffering, before reinforcing his original point with a further brief comment at the end.

Dialogue

Dialogue is the use of direct speech, showing us what the characters say and the interactions between them, rather than telling us about it as past-tense reported speech. So it makes the narrative more immediate and in fact shares several features with plays, because each speaker has a distinctive voice.

Consider this key moment in *Alive* by Piers Paul Read.

> 'It's not going to be easy getting out of here,' said Canessa.
>
> 'But if we aren't rescued, we'll have to walk out,' said Fito.
>
> 'We'd never make it,' said Canessa. 'Look how weak we've become without food.'
>
> 'Do you know what Nando said to me?' Carlitos said to Fito. 'He said that if we weren't rescued he'd eat one of the pilots to get out of here.' There was a pause; then Carlitos added, 'That hit on the head must have made him slightly mad.'
>
> 'I don't know,' said Fito, his honest, serious features quite composed. 'It might be the only way to survive.'

 Key terms

Dialogue: direct speech between two or more characters in a narrative. It normally imitates some but not all of the features of real-life talk.

This could have been expressed as: 'The boys began to realise that if they were going to survive they would have to eat some of the corpses.' However, the use of dialogue has made it much stronger.

Very few people can remember the exact words someone used even two minutes later, let alone after a long lapse of time, and dialogue is always tidied up, with accidental repetitions, hesitations and false starts left out. There is always some element of fiction in the representation of speech, however realistic it looks, but this is an accepted convention. Read points out what he has done in the acknowledgements at the beginning of the text, where he says: 'With the exception of rendering some speech in dialogue form, nothing in this book departs from the truth as it was told to me by those involved.'

You will find that most writers of non-fiction use a good deal of dialogue because it makes the narrative more lively and more dramatic. In fact, this is one of the techniques that can blur the distinction between the two, because all dialogue is shaped and edited by the author. In real life, people very rarely, if ever, talk as clearly and succinctly as they do in books.

In fiction, writers often present a great deal of their material as dialogue, for realistic effect and to develop character and theme.

Realism in dialogue

 Critical response activity

Consider the way J. G. Ballard represents speech in the following extract from *Empire of the Sun*.

Jim (aged ten) has wandered away from his parents and has lost his model plane in Lunghua airfield, which is just being invaded by Japanese soldiers. His father realises Jim is in great danger and comes to bring the boy back, telling him to leave the plane.

■ How does Ballard make it sound realistic?

■ What tells you that this is speech in a novel, not a transcript of an actual conversation?

Jim could see that it was an effort for his father to speak. His face was as strained and bloodless as it had been when the labour organizers at the mill threatened to kill him. Yet he was still thinking about something. 'We'll leave it for the soldiers – finders keepers.'

'Like kites?'

'That's it.'

'He wasn't very angry.'

'It looks as if they're waiting for something to happen.'

'The next war?'

'I don't suppose so.'

Hand in hand they walked across the airfield. Nothing moved except for the ceaselessly rippling grass, rehearsing itself for the slipstreams to come. When they reached the hangar his father tightly embraced Jim, almost trying to hurt him, as if Jim had been lost to him forever.

This sounds very casual and natural, with its **elisions** such as 'wasn't', 'they're' and 'don't'. It uses **ellipsis**, such as 'The next war?', where some of the meaning is implied rather than stated, as we often do in conversation. The **colloquial** expression 'finders keepers' is one that is appropriate in talking to a boy, but would be unusual in more formal contexts. However, this conversation is more condensed than actual speech normally is. No word is wasted.

Ballard does not tell us that the father is desperately afraid for his son's safety; he shows us this in the hug he gives Jim when they reach the hangar. Similarly, the short utterances in the conversation show tension very economically. There are no hesitations or false starts, and they imply far more than is actually said. 'The next war?' suggests the imminent invasion of Shanghai.

Dialect

Not all speech is Standard English. There are also many varieties of **dialect**, each with its own rules of grammar and vocabulary. Writers often use these to show us where a character comes from, or to suggest his or her social class, or both.

Critical response activity

This extract comes from *North and South*. The speaker is the daughter of one of the leaders of a strike.

- What are the main differences here from Standard English?
- Why does Gaskell choose to make her speak in this dialect?

They were to hou'd together through thick and thin; what the major part thought, t'others were to think, whether they would or no. And above all there was to be no going again the law of the land. Folk would go with them if they saw them striving and starving wi' dumb patience; but if there was once any noise o' fighting and struggling – even wi' knobsticks – all was up, as they knew by th'experience of many, and many a time before. They would try and get speech o' th' knobsticks, and coax 'em, and reason wi' 'em, and m'appen warn 'em off; but whatever came, Committee charged all members o' th' Union to lie down and die, if need were, without striking a blow; and then they reckoned they were sure o' carrying th' public with them.

Commentary

There are several characteristic features of dialect here.

- One of the first things you may notice about this are the pronunciation features – the elisions such as 'hou'd' for 'hold' or 'wi'' for 'with'. These give us the sound of the speaker's accent. However, it is perfectly possible to speak Standard English with a regional accent.
- There is also some special vocabulary, such as 'knobsticks', which means 'blacklegs', people who work during a strike. *North and South* contains a short glossary of dialect words at the end, some of which may be completely unfamiliar.
- 'Get speech of' and 'm'appen' ('may happen' – 'perhaps') are grammatical constructions that are characteristic of this dialect.

Bessy Higgins, the speaker here, comes from a working-class background and has lived all her life in Milton-Northern (based on Manchester).

Key terms

Elision: the running together of words or the omission of parts of words – for example, 'don't' for 'do not' or 'y'know' for 'you know'.

Ellipsis: the omission of part of a sentence, which is then understood from the context. 'Hope you get well soon' is an example of ellipsis where the pronoun 'I' has been left out. An ellipsis is sometimes represented by three dots (...) to indicate the missing part of a sentence.

Colloquial: language that may be used in ordinary conversation but is not appropriate in formal or literary contexts.

Dialect: a variety of a particular language characterised by distinctive features of accent, grammar and vocabulary, used by people from a geographical area or social group.

Think about it

When you come to work on the creative writing part of your coursework, you will be limited as to word count, but you will probably want to use dialogue for its dramatic effect, and because it gives variety to the narrative. If you plan carefully, just a few words of direct speech can carry a lot of information.

Giving her this kind of localised language makes the character sound more realistic. You will notice, though, that what she says is thoughtful and logical. She gives a clear and full explanation of the strike leaders' thinking. Being a dialect speaker does not in itself reflect on a character's intelligence, even though some writers appear to assume such a link.

In *The Adventures of Huckleberry Finn* Mark Twain gives a dazzlingly brilliant rendering of a number of American dialects, explaining that: 'The shadings have not been done in a haphazard fashion, or by guesswork; but painstakingly, and with the trustworthy guidance and support of personal familiarity with these forms of speech.'

The most extreme of these dialects belongs to Jim, the Negro, whose speech is sometimes used for comic effect, such as when Huck and Tom Sawyer, up to mischief, are standing near him in the dark without speaking. Jim says:

> 'Say – who is you? Whar is you? Dog my cats ef I disn' hear sumf'n. Well, I knows what I's gwyne to do. I's gwyne to set down here and listen tell I hears it agin.'

AQA Examiner's tip

Though you are likely to want to use direct speech in your creative work, writing dialect is not something to be undertaken lightly, as Mark Twain points out. Only use regional or historical speech in your own writing if you really do have expert knowledge about its rules and patterns, or it will sound false.

5   How do writers represent character?

There is a close connection between theme and the presentation of character. After plot, this is the earliest feature of narrative that most readers will become aware of. Quite often characters become so popular that there is a demand for more stories about them. Arthur Conan Doyle famously tried to kill off Sherlock Holmes in one of his adventures, but was forced by disappointed readers to bring him back to life. Raymond Chandler's Philip Marlowe is the hero of a whole series of novels, and this is the case for many other detectives created by crime writers.

Many features contribute to the creation of character, some of them small details, some of them involving complex psychology. Language features include:

- choice of names
- descriptive detail of appearance
- characters' speech patterns.

Names

Names are an important part of identity and carry all kinds of **connotations** of age, status, nationality or personality.

- Often writers will choose names that indicate the characteristics of the person described. The hero and heroine of *The Woman in White* are called Walter Hartright and Laura Fairlie, names which have positive connotations of courage and beauty. The villain is called Sir Percival Glyde, which suggests untrustworthiness.

- Only two characters have personal names in *Heart of Darkness* – Marlow the narrator, and Mr Kurtz the main subject. Other characters in the framework narrative have generic names, some with capital letters, such as the 'Director of Companies' or the 'Accountant'. In Marlow's main narrative, a group of characters employed by the trading company have the ironic name of 'pilgrims' because 'they wandered here and there with their absurd long staves in their hands like a lot of faithless pilgrims bewitched inside a rotten fence'. No African has a personal name at all. The effect of this is to create the sense of a hierarchy of importance within the characters in the story.

- Names and forms of address indicate social class. In *North and South* characters of social standing have courtesy titles, such as Mr Hale, Mr Thornton. Nicholas Higgins, as a worker, is usually referred to as 'Higgins'. Dixon, the Hale family servant, has no forename at all, as was the custom of the times, even though she is an important member of the household.

- In *Testament of Youth* Vera Brittain changes or abbreviates a number of the names to conceal the identity of real people.

This chapter covers:

- awareness of names, descriptive detail and speech in characterisation
- analysis of character revealed through action
- considering the reader's judgement.

AQA   Examiner's tip

When you are writing about a text always make a special effort to check that you have spelled the names of the author and the characters correctly. Careless presentation of names is one of the things that needlessly creates a bad impression.

Key terms

Connotations: the associations that words evoke in the mind of the reader in addition to their basic meanings. For example, there is a difference between 'house', which suggests a building, and 'home', which suggests a place where people live.

Practical activity

Try changing the names in an extract from the text you have been studying. Does it have an effect?

Many names have connotations of age, social class or group identity and the result of changing these can be very interesting. Would you call a modest character Isidor Ottavio Baldassare Fosco? What would happen to the tone of your narrative if you changed this name to Jack White, for example?

Descriptions of appearance

The third-person narrative has an advantage in the matter of description. It can tell us what the main character looks like from the outside. First-person narratives can easily enough describe other characters when the main protagonist meets them, but have more difficulty in presenting actual portraits of the hero or heroine.

In fiction, there is a tendency to draw comparisons between the physical appearance of characters and their psychology. For instance, there is often a strong inclination to make a connection between beauty and goodness, and writers are quite well aware that their audience will expect this. Few physical descriptions are without bias.

■ Critical response activity

Wilkie Collins plays with the convention of making a connection between physical appearance and psychology in *The Woman in White*. Here is the first description of Marian Halcombe. The speaker is Walter Hartright.

How is Collins teasing the reader here?

> I looked from the table to the window farthest from me, and saw a lady standing at it, with her back towards me. The instant my eyes rested on her, I was struck by the rare beauty of her form, and by the unaffected grace of her attitude. Her figure was tall, yet not too tall; comely and well-developed, yet not fat; her head set on her shoulders with an easy, pliant firmness; her waist, perfection in the eyes of a man, for it occupied its natural place, it filled out its natural circle, it was visibly and delightfully undeformed by stays. She had not heard my entrance into the room; and I allowed myself the luxury of admiring her for a few moments, before I moved one of the chairs near me, as the least embarrassing means of attracting her attention. She turned towards me immediately. The easy elegance of every movement of her limbs and body as soon as she began to advance from the far end of the room set me in a flutter of expectation to see her face clearly. She left the window – and I said to myself, The lady is dark. She moved forward a few steps – and I said to myself, The lady is young. She approached nearer – and I said to myself (with a sense of surprise which words fail me to express), The lady is ugly!

Commentary

Poor Marian has a moustache and a firm jaw! She is not the heroine, and plays a somewhat masculine part in the action. The narrator goes on to comment that she does not have the 'feminine attractions of gentleness and pliability'.

This is near the beginning of the novel, where Hartright, the hero, has not yet met Laura, the woman he will fall in love with. Collins teases us by giving a very detailed physical description of Marian's figure, but only gradually revealing the most important part – her face. Notice all the phrases in praise of her: 'rare beauty', 'comely and well-developed' and 'easy, pliant firmness'. Then he moves on in a series of short, parallel and emphatic statements from 'The lady is dark' and 'The lady is young' – both neutral in judgement – to 'The lady is ugly!', which is emphasised by the exclamation mark. This comes as a complete surprise and immediately alters the way we see the relationship between the two characters.

■ Practical activity

In two columns, make a list of characters in fiction, one of heroes and the other of villains (not necessarily in novels – they could be from films or television series). Now put a tick by all the ones that are good-looking and a cross by all the ones who are physically unattractive. Does this show anything?

With a first-person narrative it is more difficult to give physical descriptions. Details about the author's appearance are more likely to be scattered through the body of the text rather than given as a set piece at the beginning. For different reasons, two narrators, Holden Caulfield, in fiction, and George Orwell, in real life, both tell us that they are unusually tall. This comes out in the context: Holden can sometimes buy alcoholic drinks because people think he is older than he really is; Orwell suffers agonies in the cramped spaces of a coal mine he visits to watch the miners at work.

■ Practical activity

Select passages from your set texts where characters are introduced for the first time and underline the adjectives used to describe them.

How much does this suggest about the role they will play in the narrative as a whole?

Clothes can sometimes be an indicator of both appearance and character. Several times in her autobiography, *Testament of Youth*, Vera Brittain associates an important moment with clothes. For example, she writes of a meeting with her fiancé, Roland, who was later killed in the war.

> I longed to look at him closely and yet was too shy: his uniform and little moustache had changed him from a boy into a man, and one so large and powerful that even in the splendour of the rose-trimmed hat and a new squirrel coat given me by my father I felt like a midget beside him.

■ Critical response activity

Here is a detail from the ending of *Testament of Youth*, where a much older Vera Brittain struggles to board a moving train to meet her future husband, known only as 'G'.

What effect does she achieve from the description here?

> I scrambled, regardless of the dove-coloured coat-frock and new terra-cotta hat, up the steep step from the dirty siding. Completely ruining my pale suede gloves with the coal dust on the grimy handle, I opened the nearest door and fell into the corridor ...

Commentary

On one level, being prepared to ruin her clothes shows the importance of the occasion and Brittain's energetic approach. On another level, the detailed description, full of adjectives – 'dove-coloured', 'terra-cotta', 'pale suede' – shows how much value she attaches to her smart and feminine appearance.

Key terms

Idiolect: the language characteristics of an individual speaker, including choice of vocabulary and idiom, grammar and pronunciation.

Spoken words

Many characters have individual styles of speech, personal to them. (This may sometimes include the use of dialect, as we discussed in Chapter 4.) The technical name for speech patterns that are especially characteristic of one person is **idiolect**.

In *The Catcher in the Rye*, J. D. Salinger imitates a slangy, teenage style of language throughout, suitable for Holden Caulfield's age and the spontaneity of his narrative.

David Lodge calls Holden Caulfield 'a literary descendant of Huck Finn'. In *The Art of Fiction* he gives a detailed analysis of a passage from *The Catcher in the Rye* as an example of 'Teenage *Skatz*'. Lodge points out that, although this style gives an impression of authenticity and truthfulness through its use of idiolect, it is actually 'the product of much calculated effort and painstaking writing by the "real" author'.

The novel as a whole shows Holden as an anxious and uncertain character, appalled by the snobbish, hypocritical and unscrupulous behaviour of those around him. Many of the repetitions in his speech reflect this, while his constant exaggeration shows his emotional turbulence.

He uses mainly short, uncomplicated sentences, which sound like real speech. To make him sound like a teenager, Salinger gives him frequent slang expressions such as 'big deal', 'killed me' and 'old'. Throughout the narrative other characters keep telling Holden not to swear. In fact his constant use of language such as 'goddam' and 'bastard' caused considerable offence when the book first came out.

Making your own judgement

Of course, we do not necessarily have to take what a character says simply at face value. The presentation may be ironic. All readers bring their own set of values to a text, affecting the way they respond to it. We are often conscious of the narrator's voice too, as we discussed in Chapter 3.

AQA **Examiner's tip**

The characters in fiction are not real people and have no life outside what the author chooses to describe. In analysis it is important to realise this.

In creative writing, however, *you* are the author and can invent as much as you like as long as your invention is reasonably convincing. You can describe events from a different point of view, using characters with completely different attitudes. When you do this, remember your audience. Do not use language that your intended audience might find offensive, even if it is realistic.

Critical response activity

Consider this extract from *The Adventures of Huckleberry Finn*. Tom Sawyer, on a visit to his Aunt Sally, has just joined up with Huck, who is trying to liberate the negro slave Jim from captivity. This is theft, as slaves are valuable property. Huck speaks first here.

Can you disentangle the likely moral positions of:

■ Huck?
■ Tom Sawyer?
■ the reader?

'There's a nigger that I'm trying to steal out of slavery – and his name is *Jim* – old Miss Watson's Jim.'

He says:

'What! Why Jim is –'

He stopped and went to studying. I says:

'*I* know what you'll say. You'll say it's a dirty low-down business; but what if it is? – I'm low down; and I'm a-going to steal him, and I want you to keep mum and not let on. Will you?'

His eye lit up and he says:

'I'll *help* you steal him!'

Well, I let go all holts then, like I was shot. It was the most astonishing speech I ever heard – and I'm bound to say Tom Sawyer fell, considerable, in my estimation. Only I couldn't believe it. Tom Sawyer a *nigger stealer*!

Commentary

■ Huck wants to help Jim, who has become his friend, and is prepared to commit a crime in order to do so. At the same time, he is aware that he is breaking a moral code, and feels some guilt about it. He is astonished that Tom Sawyer, whom he knows to be 'respectable and well-brung up', is actually prepared to join him in a serious theft.

■ Tom Sawyer knows that Jim is not in fact a slave at this point, having already been given his freedom. He is about to reveal this in the phrase 'Why Jim is –' and then thinks better of it. He sees the opportunity to turn the rescue of Jim into a romantic game, without telling Huck the real situation.

■ The reader is unlikely to approve of slavery, and will probably see Huck's plan to rescue Jim as evidence of good intentions rather than a lack of morals.

Actions and habits

When you first looked at plot, as distinct from story, you were actually also starting to think about character because the two are so closely connected. If 'the queen died of grief' is a plot, then we already have some idea of the kind of person the queen was – she must have been capable of deep emotion. Action both develops and reflects character; it operates on both the large scale and the small.

Plot and character are closely intertwined. In the previous extract from *The Adventures of Huckleberry Finn*, the character of Tom Sawyer drives the plot. Sawyer, who has a rich, imaginative inner life, never misses the opportunity to turn everyday reality into the kind of wild adventure he reads about in books. Here Huck describes an absurd moment from the 'rescue' of Jim:

Then we started for the house, and I went in the back door – you only have to pull a buckskin latch-string, they don't fasten the doors – but that warn't romantical enough for Tom Sawyer: no way would do him but he must climb up the lightning rod. But after he got up half-way about three times, and missed fire and fell every time, and the last time most busted his brains out, he thought he'd got to give it up; but after he was rested, he allowed he would give her one more turn for luck, and this time he made the trip.

Think about it

How many of the characters in each of the texts you are studying actually develop so that your opinions about them change during the course of the narrative?

In what ways do they develop?

Think about it

Developing fictional characters so that they grow and change normally requires space, and is more commonly associated with novels than with short stories. In real life people do naturally change in response to their experience as they get older, so you would expect biographical writing to reflect this.

What sorts of circumstances or events might lead to change or a new sense of values?

Sometimes small actions, with little relevance to the main thrust of the plot, can be used to define character. Count Fosco, the fat villain in *The Woman in White*, is characterised by his habit of drinking sugar water and playing with his pet white mice, the apparent childishness of these actions contrasting with his deep and ruthless scheming.

Characters who change and develop

In fiction, many characters are dynamic and develop as the plot progresses. E. M. Forster makes a well-known distinction here between 'flat' and 'round' characters. 'Flat' ones can often be summed up in a phrase, or are seen purely from the outside. 'Round' characters have an inner life. Once this happens, they become capable of change, for better or worse. Holden Caulfield progresses towards his breakdown; Margaret Hale loses her snobbish prejudices against 'trade' and comes to understand both John Thornton and the world of commerce.

In *Heart of Darkness*, Joseph Conrad achieves a particularly subtle balance of 'showing' and 'telling', as the narrator and other characters provide comment on the continual development of the 'remarkable' Mr Kurtz and the 'magnificent folds of eloquence' that hide 'the barren darkness of his heart'.

Conrad avoids giving the detail of Kurtz's speeches, leaving them to the imagination. Eventually the 'unextinguishable gift of lofty and noble expression' that his admirers describe degenerates into the insight contained in his brief final words: 'The horror! The horror!'

6   How does setting contribute to the writer's themes?

The appeal of setting is strong. If readers want to hear more and more of a character they are familiar with, the same often applies to locations. There is a particular pleasure in reading about life in places different from where we live; this is one of the ways in which literature can enlarge our experience. It does not mean that such places are always agreeable; the mean streets of Philip Marlowe's world create as evocative a background as any other. They are the appropriate setting for Chandler's characters.

Sometimes in the literature of travel the setting for a work is virtually the theme – for example, in Tim Butcher's exploration of the Congo in *Blood River*; and in *Robinson Crusoe* and *Alive*, where survival in a hostile setting provides the main subject matter of the book.

You may be familiar with L. P. Hartley's **epigram**, 'The past is a foreign country: they do things differently there.' Time, as well as place, is an aspect of narrative setting.

Locating the action in fiction

There is only a limited number of basic story patterns, but an infinite number of settings. David Lodge points out that the sense of place 'was a fairly late development in the history of prose fiction'. Robinson Crusoe, whose environment on his island is so important, is mainly interested in facts about food or shelter. In most modern fiction the setting plays a very important part in distinguishing one narrative from another and in creating atmosphere. Detectives, for instance, usually have a clear territory in which they operate. Remember Raymond Chandler's third commandment for the detective story: 'It must be realistic in character, setting, and atmosphere. It must be about real people in a real world.'

Critical response activity

In the following extract from *The Lady in the Lake*, Raymond Chandler describes Marlowe's first meeting with his client, Derace Kingsley.

- What does this description of Kingsley's office tell us about his background?
- What do you deduce about Marlowe from his reaction to this setting?
- What do you notice about the contribution of sense impressions in this extract?

> The private office was everything a private office should be. It was long and dim and quiet and air-conditioned and its windows were shut and its grey Venetian blinds half-closed to keep out the July glare. Grey drapes matched the grey carpeting. There was a large black and silver safe in the corner and a low row of filing cases that exactly matched it. On the wall there was a huge tinted photograph of an elderly party with a chiselled beak and whiskers and a wing collar. The Adam's apple that edged through his wing collar looked harder than most people's chins. The plate underneath the photograph read: *Mr Matthew Gillerlain, 1860–1934.*

This chapter covers:

- being aware of different ways of presenting setting in fiction
- recognising the importance of descriptions of place in non-fiction
- historical settings.

Key terms

Epigram: a pithy saying or remark that sums up an idea.

Think about it

One of the ways in which you might approach the creative writing section of your coursework is by altering the setting in time and place of a story and moving it into a modern context. What kind of changes in the characters' general way of life would this involve?

Further reading

David Lodge, *The Art of Fiction*, Penguin, 1994

> Derace Kingsley marched briskly behind about eight hundred dollars' worth of executive desk and planted his backside in a tall leather chair. He reached himself a panatela out of a copper and mahogany box and lit it with a fat copper desk lighter. He took his time about it. It didn't matter about my time.

Commentary

This description, very near the opening of the novel, is typical of Chandler in its precision and close attention to detail. The fittings such as the large safe and 'about eight hundred dollars' worth of executive desk' realistically convey an impression of wealth and power in Marlowe's client. It is also a calm scene, 'dim and quiet' with its 'half-closed' blinds and grey tones, indicating an owner who does not wish to be personally disturbed by any outside unpleasantness.

Marlowe is unimpressed by all this opulence. We know this from his comic description of the photograph. He refers to Gillerlain, clearly the firm's founder, as 'an elderly party'. He also tells us, disrespectfully, how Kingsley 'planted his backside' in the chair. One of the themes here is that of the detective as shrewd observer, noticing all kinds of information and making independent judgements.

Sense impressions are important in descriptive writing. Chandler tells us what the office looks like, but he also appeals to other senses: to that of touch when he tells us that it is 'air-conditioned' and cool, and to hearing because it is 'quiet'. You might bear this in mind as we consider other examples of descriptive writing.

Place and atmosphere

Weather and landscape play a part in setting the mood in many novels, even seeming to be an integral part of the action. The Victorian critic John Ruskin, who disliked this literary effect, described it as 'a falseness in … impressions of external things which I would generally characterize as the "**pathetic fallacy**"', and the name has stuck. It does not necessarily imply sadness, although the scenes described are often sad enough; a bright spring day might be the background for a very cheerful story.

■ **Think about it**

Try to be aware of sense impressions in your own creative writing. Touch and smell are particularly evocative of atmosphere.

■ **Key terms**

Pathetic fallacy: the literary technique of suggesting human states and emotions through the description of details such as landscape and weather. For example, a writer might use a dreary setting on a rainy day to suggest that a character is feeling sad. It is a 'fallacy' because inanimate surroundings cannot really respond to human feelings except in the imagination.

■ **Critical response activity**

Look at the following description from *The Woman in White* of Blackwater Park, the home of the villainous Sir Percival Glyde.

■ How does Collins create an impression of loneliness and decay?

■ Why does the place seem dangerous?

■ Can you suggest why the author creates this mood? What kind of action is Collins preparing us for by the use of this setting?

> The ground, shelving away below me, was all sand, with a few little heathy hillocks to break the monotony of it in certain places. The lake itself had evidently once flowed to the spot on which I stood, and had been gradually wasted and dried up to less than a third of its former size. I saw its still, stagnant waters, a quarter of a mile away from me in the hollow, separated into pools and ponds by twining reeds and rushes, and little knolls of earth. On the farther bank from me the trees rose thickly again, and shut out the view, and cast their black shadows on the sluggish, shallow water. As I walked down to the lake, I saw that the ground on its

farther side was damp and marshy, overgrown with rank grass and dismal willows. The water, which was clear enough on the sandy side, where the sun shone, looked black and poisonous opposite to me, where it lay deeper under the shade of the spongy banks, and the rank overhanging thickets and tangled trees. The frogs were croaking, and the rats were slipping in and out of the shadowy water, like live shadows themselves, as I got nearer to the marshy side of the lake. I saw there, lying half in and half out of the water, the rotten wreck of an overturned boat, with a sickly spot of sunlight glimmering through a gap in the trees on its dry surface, and a snake basking in the midst of the spot, fantastically coiled and treacherously still.

Commentary

- The narrator (Marian Halcombe) moves out of sunlight towards ominous darkness in the passage. The landscape appears to close in. The lake itself has 'gradually wasted and dried up' showing that the park has not been maintained and cared for; few people are likely to come to such a neglected place, so it is lonely and threatening. The boat is a 'rotten wreck', suggesting that it has been a long time since anyone used the lake for pleasure.

- Collins introduces descriptive details that stress danger. The 'tangled trees' suggest possible hiding places for anyone lurking there. The adjectives 'stagnant' and 'poisonous' convey the unhealthy nature of the water. Even the sunlight is 'sickly', not strong and healthy. Readers are likely to be repelled by the kind of animals found there, rats and a snake. The snake seems particularly threatening because it is 'treacherously still'.

- Collins intends this as a suitable setting for villainy and the theme of lurking secrets. The reason the place is so neglected is because Sir Percival Glyde, its owner, is desperately short of money. The darkness and the treacherous snake are symbolic of threats to the heroine, who has no easy means of escape. This gloomy old house at Blackwater Park has suggestions of **Gothic horror**. Even the place name seems intended to be dark and threatening.

> **Key terms**
>
> **Gothic horror:** a style of fiction that stresses mystery and extreme emotional reaction.

This description is very different from Chandler's, but notice once again that we learn about the sounds of the place, with the frogs 'croaking' and the suggestion of touch in the 'damp' ground. The appeal to the senses brings the description to life.

Real locations

Both fiction and non-fiction texts may describe real places. *Alive* and *Blood River* both provide helpful maps of their locations, but so does *Empire of the Sun*, which is a novel based on real wartime experience and what Ballard called his '13-year-old's infatuation with the war'. He has fictionalised the actual circumstances of his internment by leaving out his parents, but the descriptions of place are completely authentic.

Some descriptions of setting are necessarily factual. The whole point of *Alive* is that the young men are trapped high in the Andes well above the snowline. A crucial problem hampering the rescue attempts was that the pilot gave an inaccurate description of the plane's position immediately before it crashed. Attempts at finding out exactly where the survivors had come down are central to the structure of the book.

Blood River belongs to the genre of travel literature and is organised mainly by the way we follow the author's journey; in this case its author calls it 'ordeal travel' because of the extreme difficulties involved. Butcher follows the route of the American explorer, Henry Morton Stanley, who mapped the River Congo in 1874.

■ Critical response activity

Butcher describes the terrain in detail in the short extract below. What do you think is Butcher's main purpose in describing scenes like the one given here?

Is this just a literal description or does the writer see a wider significance in the scene?

> Benoit shouted to take care as he picked his way past holes in the planking of the bridge, but I wanted to stop and walk around. The girders were brown with rust but, to my layman's eye, they seemed sound and functional. The bridge stood ten metres above the water, so was clear of the threat of being washed away by floodwaters. But what struck me was the folly it represented. A solid bridge capable of carrying heavy trucks and traffic had been designed, built, brought here and eventually assembled on the assumption that heavy trucks and traffic would be able to reach it. Since the Belgians left the Congo, that assumption had collapsed, so there the bridge stands, a memorial deep in the jungle to the folly of planners who never dreamed that the Congo would spiral backwards as much as it has.

Commentary

This paragraph of description is typical of many scenes in the book where Butcher records the decay of the whole country and its collapsing infrastructure, noting burnt-out villages and dilapidated houses as typical features along his route. The bridge becomes not just an example but also a symbol of 'folly' and mismanagement. Although decaying, it has so far stood up against the forces of nature, but not against human stupidity.

He wants to bring out the way everything has been allowed to 'spiral backwards' in the post-colonial era, a major theme throughout his narrative. Over and over again he gives concrete examples of the effects of violence and corruption on the life of the country, as he describes the places he passes through.

Time

Time, as well as place, is an important aspect of the setting of any narrative, especially when major historical events form part of the action. This is not always immediately obvious. *The Adventures of Huckleberry Finn*, for instance, calls on recent memories of slavery, but the book itself was written nearly twenty years after the end of the American Civil War. A strictly contemporary Jim would not have been a slave, and therefore a piece of property, in 1884, which makes a subtle difference to the reader's reactions. In your study, you need to be aware of historical context, especially in the ways society has changed economically and politically.

Two of the most important aspects of Vera Brittain's autobiography are:

■ her personal experiences of the First World War

■ the rise of feminism in the early part of the twentieth century.

Her book has become valuable source material about the ways in which historical events affected individual lives at the time.

Critical response activity

Here is a short extract from Vera Brittain's description of her time as a student at Oxford in 1915. How does she bring out the background to this personal account?

> The day after Rupert Brooke's death in the Aegean, and a few hours before the Allied landing at Cape Helles on April 25th, I returned for the last term of my first year to an Oxford that now seemed infinitely remote from everything that counted. During the vacation, Somerville College, adjacent as it was to the Radcliffe Infirmary, had been commandeered by the War Office for conversion into a military hospital.

Commentary

Vera Brittain's emotional life takes up a great deal of space in her autobiography. However, the events of the war – here she refers to Rupert Brooke's death and the Allied landing in Gallipoli – are intertwined with her personal experiences as an undergraduate. Factual information about the use of buildings in Oxford gives a framework to her reactions. This switching from the wider context to her personal concerns gives a strong indication of what it actually felt like to live through these circumstances. After the war, the same kind of thing happens with her reactions to the changing role of women. She writes, for example:

> From the moment that the War ended I had always known, and my parents had always tolerantly taken for granted, that after three years at Oxford and four of wartime adventure, my return to a position of subservient dependence at home would be tolerable neither for them nor for me.

George Orwell's study of life in the north of England in the 1930s gives a detailed account of work in the mining industry at that time, a way of life that has long since disappeared. You might need to consider whether the passage of time has affected the force of his arguments about the value of socialism.

Although it is a novel, *Empire of the Sun* also reliably describes important historical events of the Second World War, from the time of the Japanese attack on Pearl Harbor, through the dropping of the atomic bombs on Hiroshima and Nagasaki, to the eventual American liberation of Shanghai in 1945. You might think about the ways in which the authentic historical background affects your attitude to the ways in which the characters are presented.

Think about it.

General historical background could be of great use in your own creative work. If you are writing an extra chapter for one of the Victorian novels, for example, you might think carefully about details of setting, such as what most buildings were like at the time.

Some features of linguistic tone: persuasion, humour and symbolism

This chapter covers:

- considering some effects of different purposes in writing

- analysing different kinds of humour

- noting the way symbols may express themes.

The selection of set novels and literary non-fiction includes writing with a wide variety of purposes – entertainment, information and persuasion among them. All these involve different techniques. Each writer's main purpose will naturally affect the tone of the narrative, and so influence the way the various themes are presented to the reader.

The aspects of language discussed here under different headings are not mutually exclusive; a persuasive piece may well make use of humour or symbolism in its argument, just as a novel will often contain factual information. *The Road to Wigan Pier*, for example, famously ends with a witty expression, combining both humour and persuasion. Orwell hopes that under socialism class prejudice will eventually fade away and the middle classes will find, like him, that 'we have nothing to lose but our aitches'.

Persuasive argument

Both *The Road to Wigan Pier* and *Blood River* take up controversial positions. Both have specific political comments to make and need to convince the reader of the sound observations and arguments in their commentary.

Orwell's main purpose in *The Road to Wigan Pier* is to propose socialism as an answer to some of the country's social and economic problems, those which became particularly acute during the Depression. He begins his book with some detailed descriptions of working-class life in the north of England and then includes aspects of his own biography. This is so that the reader will understand the background from which he approaches a political position. Having established all this, three-quarters of the way through the book, he begins on his major theme, the necessity for socialism as 'a way out' because it is 'elementary common sense'.

Critical response activity

Here is an extract from *The Road to Wigan Pier*, taken from the point where Orwell suggests his political solution. The first sentence here begins a new chapter of the book.

- Consider the way Orwell begins to present the argument for socialism in this extract.

- What methods does he use to persuade his reader of the necessity for political action?

Meanwhile what about Socialism?

It hardly needs pointing out that at this moment we are in a very serious mess, so serious that even the dullest-witted people find it difficult to remain unaware of it. We are living in a world in which nobody is free, in which hardly anybody is secure, in which it is almost impossible to be honest and to remain alive. For enormous blocks of the working class the conditions of life are such as I have described in the opening chapters of this book, and there is no chance of those conditions showing any fundamental improvement. The very best the English working class can hope for is an occasional temporary decrease in unemployment when this or that industry is artificially stimulated by, for instance, rearmament. Even the middle classes, for the first time in their history, are feeling the pinch. They have not known actual hunger yet, but more and more of them find themselves floundering in a sort of deadly net of frustration in which it is harder and harder to persuade yourself that you are either happy, active, or useful. Even the lucky ones at the top, the real bourgeoisie, are haunted periodically by a consciousness of the miseries below, and still more by fears of the menacing future. And this is merely a preliminary stage, in a country still rich with the loot of a hundred years. Presently there may be coming God knows what horrors – horrors of which, in this sheltered island, we have not even a traditional knowledge.

Commentary

Orwell opens his new chapter with a question, to which the rest of the book will provide an answer. The first four words stand alone in his opening paragraph for emphasis, inviting the reader to consider the problem. Then he brings everybody in by the use of the pronoun 'we' in the beginning of the next paragraph. Nobody wishes to be thought dull-witted, so he assumes that everyone will accept his opening statement that 'we are in a very serious mess'.

He then makes a number of assertions, based on the evidence of the earlier chapters, that there is no chance of improvement for the working class, and that the middle classes are 'feeling the pinch'.

Orwell's language here has some of the features that you would expect in a good political speech – for instance, the highly patterned threefold repetition of 'in which' in the sentence beginning 'We are living in a world …'. There is considerable emotional language, such as 'free', 'secure', 'honest', 'hunger' and 'miseries'. The word 'horrors' is repeated for emphasis. The metaphor of people 'floundering' like fish in a 'deadly net of frustration' creates an image of helplessness, while the further metaphor in 'haunted' suggests fear.

Orwell uses high-level, even mildly technical, vocabulary, such as 'artificially stimulated by … rearmament', suitable for a serious political discussion. At the same time, there is an echo of the speaking voice in down-to-earth phrases such as 'feeling the pinch' and 'God knows what', which stop the tone from becoming too abstract and remote from the reader. As with his use of the pronoun 'we' in the opening of the paragraph, the more colloquial phrases are a way of making the audience feel included.

Orwell offers socialism as a solution to difficulties. In *Blood River*, Tim Butcher, like Orwell a serious journalist with wide experience, is concerned with analysing the problems of post-colonial Africa. He gives well-informed accounts of the violence and corruption that have afflicted the Congo. One of his methods of raising issues is to link them to the personal experience of people he meets on his journey.

■ Critical response activity

The following extract is the observation of Ali, the Malaysian skipper of the boat in which Butcher is travelling. They are discussing the problems of the Congo, its dereliction and poverty.

What techniques does Butcher use to raise an important point in this extract?

> 'Malaysia was colonised for centuries too, most recently by the British, a colonial rule that was cruel and racist. We got independence at roughly the same time as the Congo in the early 1960s, and we were even drawn into a Cold War conflict for year after year as communist insurgents fought for control of Malaysia. But somehow Malaysia got through it and the Congo did not. Today, Malaysia is part of the rest of the world. People go on holiday in Malaysia. The world's business community does business in Malaysia. We even have a Grand Prix every year in Malaysia. The same is not true of the Congo. How can you explain the difference?'

Commentary

The point here is to make a contrast between the lost potential of the Congo and the present reality.

As he frequently does, Butcher uses a conversation with those who help him on his journey to make a point about the conditions of life in the Congo. Ali's opinion in this anecdote is particularly valuable because his own native country has had similar problems to those of Africa in the post-colonial era, but the outcomes have been different. No reason for the difference is offered here, merely the evidence, and readers are left to draw their own conclusions.

Ali's speech is made persuasive by its patterning, with the threefold repetition; 'People go on holiday', 'The world's business community does business' and 'We even have a Grand Prix' – all ending emphatically 'in Malaysia' to stress the fundamental contrast with the Congo.

Humour

Humour is often easier to recognise than to describe and it depends a good deal for its effect on the attitudes and experience that readers bring to it. In essence, what one audience will find funny, another may think is shocking; but it is an important aspect of tone in writing and can arise out of almost any situation.

Comedy divides into many subgenres, but for simplicity we shall consider the contribution made to texts by humour of situation and of character, and verbal wit.

Comic situations

Huck Finn is always getting into scrapes. Although the circumstances are often dangerous and potentially threatening for his hero, Mark Twain emphasises the ridiculous aspects and gives Huck a thoroughly cheerful disposition. Holden Caulfield is not primarily comic; he has a complex inner life, being what E. M. Forster calls a 'round' character. Lonely and confused, he suffers too much to be completely laughable, but like Huck he is frequently caught up in ridiculous situations.

For example, there is the incident where a prostitute comes to his room, then tries to overcharge him for services he has not, in fact, received. He refuses to pay any extra money, at which point her pimp beats him up. Or there is the scene in the Lavender Room nightclub where he tries to pick up three women at the next table. The contrast between Holden's aspirations and the women's treatment of him is comic as well as pathetic.

Comic characters

Some characters in novels are presented as comic, or as caricatures, throughout. Most commonly these are the characters E. M. Forster describes as 'flat'. Seen from the outside, Professor Pesca, a minor character in *The Woman in White*, is a good example.

Critical response activity

Professor Pesca, who is very small and excitable, is an Italian friend of Hartright, who once rescued him from drowning. Collins uses him as the means of bringing about several important developments in the plot (although he takes little part in the main action himself).

In the extract below Pesca has found Hartright a job and also broken a teacup. How does Collins make the characterisation of the professor here thoroughly comic?

> Pesca, happily and fussily unconscious of the irreparable wrong which the crockery had suffered at his hands, was dragging a large armchair to the opposite end of the room, so as to command us all three, in the character of a public speaker addressing an audience. Having turned the chair with its back towards us, he jumped into it on his knees, and excitedly addressed his small congregation of three from an impromptu pulpit.
>
> 'Now, my good dears,' began Pesca (who always said 'good dears' when he meant 'worthy friends'), 'listen to me. The time has come – I recite my good news – I speak at last.'
>
> 'Hear, hear!' said my mother, humouring the joke.
>
> 'The next thing he will break, mamma,' whispered Sarah, 'will be the back of the best armchair.'
>
> 'I go back into my life, and I address the noblest of created beings,' continued Pesca, vehemently apostrophising my unworthy self over the top rail of the chair. 'Who found me dead at the bottom of the sea (through Cramp); and who pulled me up to the top; and what did I say when I got into my own life and my own clothes again?'
>
> 'Much more than was at all necessary,' I answered as doggedly as possible.

Commentary

Pesca's contribution to the actual plot here is that he sends Hartright to Limmeridge Hall. The leisurely pace of the narrative means that we do not learn this immediately, but wait while Collins derives comedy from his announcement.

We already know from an earlier chapter that Pesca is known for his 'harmless eccentricity' and this scene demonstrates it in action, with Hartright as amused narrator. Pesca is clumsy, but quite unconscious that he is wreaking havoc by breaking the crockery. Turning the chair into a 'pulpit' is a further ridiculous action.

Collins gives him the somewhat stereotypical role of the funny foreigner, with an imperfect grasp of English which leads him to use odd phrases like 'my good dears'. For instance, the exaggerated phrasing of 'the noblest of created beings' is comic, as well as the juxtaposition of 'my own life and my own clothes'.

 Link

For another thoroughly comic character see the description of Tom Sawyer on page 26.

Verbal humour

While the writers of autobiographies or travel books are unlikely to see themselves as completely comic, anyone may make a joke. Vera Brittain recounts a story of how she won over a tough audience that was heckling her. A male speaker, intending to be chivalrous, tried to come to her defence by saying, 'I can look after myself, but –' She interrupted him with 'So can I!' At this, she says, the audience 'rocked with applause and laughter.'

Serious situations in fiction may also be presented in witty language.

Critical response activity

Consider this extract from *The Lady in the Lake*. Marlowe has recently been knocked unconscious and is trying to escape from the corrupt policeman who has framed him for murder.

What is the effect of Chandler's unexpected use of comparison?

> I shut the bathroom door and stood on the edge of the tub and eased the window up. This was the sixth floor. There was no screen. I put my head out and looked into darkness and a narrow glimpse of a street with trees. I looked sideways and saw that the bathroom window of the next apartment was not more than three feet away. A well-nourished mountain goat could make it without any trouble at all.
>
> The question was whether a battered private detective could make it, and if so, what the harvest would be.

Commentary

This is characteristic of the narrator's style in several ways. There is the accurate observation of detail, the short sentences giving the story momentum and maintaining tension. The wisecrack, 'a well-nourished mountain goat could make it without any trouble at all', makes a sharp contrast, bringing an element of the absurd and the entertaining into Marlowe's predicament.

Chandler's Philip Marlowe makes deliberate jokes, but writers often include unconscious and ironic verbal humour in direct speech. In the example of Holden's adventure in the Lavender Room nightclub we looked at earlier, Salinger continues to make a comic point out of the women's accent and the lack of communication; Holden speaks first:

> 'I said did you ever hear of Marco and Miranda?'
>
> 'I don't know. No. I don't know.'
>
> 'Well, they're dancers, she's a dancer. She's not too hot though. She does everything she's supposed to, but she's not so hot anyway. You know when a girl's a really terrific dancer?'
>
> 'Wudga say?' she said. She wasn't listening to me even.

Critical response activity

Mark Twain uses his mastery of dialects for comic effect. Here is Jim's view of the wisdom of Solomon and his number of wives.

What is comic about the language here? The actual dialect forms are only part of the effect.

> 'A harem's a bo'd'n-house, I reck'n. Mos' likely dey had rackety times in de nussery. En I reck'n de wives quarrels considable; en dat 'crease de racket. Yit dey say Sollermun de wises' man dat ever live'. I doan' take no stock in dat. Bekase why: would a wise man want to live in de mids' er sich a blimblammin' all de time? No – 'deed he wouldn't. A wiser man 'ud take en buil' a biler-factry; en den he could shet down de biler-factry when he want to res.'

Commentary

Part of the effect lies in pronunciation, of course, emphasised by spelling such as 'Sollermun'. Jim's down-to-earth logic is also comic here, expressed in everyday informal vocabulary such as 'blimblammin'. He points out the likely 'racket' made in a harem, and compares it unfavourably with the noise of a mundane 'biler-factry'.

Jim is confident in questioning the biblical reputation of Solomon by applying his own logic and experience, saying 'I doan' take no stock in dat'. He conducts a dialogue with himself, asking rhetorical questions and supplying emphatic answers: 'No – 'deed he wouldn't.' (He goes on to point out that instead of the famous judgement of offering to cut the baby in half it would have been simpler to ask the neighbours for information.)

Use of symbols

Symbols are details that resonate beyond the immediate context and have a wider significance for the theme. One of the more famous moments in English literature is where Robinson Crusoe finds a footprint in the sand. Defoe uses this to mark a new phase of the novel, since it symbolises a threat from natives, whereas before Crusoe had seen no sign of human life.

In *Blood River*, the pebble that Butcher finds in his pocket at the end of his journey, and which he has carried 2,000 kilometres down the River Congo, acts as a symbol of the danger and violence of the whole journey. 'I looked at it for the final time,' he says. 'It was the colour of dried blood.' This symbol of 'the continent's bloody history' is what gives the book its title.

Key terms

Symbol: an action or object that resonates beyond its literal meaning to represent a wider idea or concept.

Critical response activity

In Joseph Conrad's *Heart of Darkness*, Marlow, the narrator, has finally reached the settlement where Kurtz has been pillaging the countryside for ivory. He tells us specifically that what he sees there is 'symbolic' and 'food for thought'.

How do you think Conrad expects us to react to this scene?

> You remember I told you I had been struck at a distance by certain attempts at ornamentation, rather remarkable in the ruinous aspect of the place. Now I had suddenly a nearer view, and its first result was to make me throw my head back as if before a blow. Then I went carefully from post to post with my glass, and I saw my mistake. These round knobs were not ornamental but symbolic; they were expressive and puzzling, striking and disturbing – food for thought and also for the vultures if there had been any looking down from the sky; but at all events for such ants as were industrious enough to ascend the pole. They would have been even more impressive, those heads on stakes, if their faces had not been turned to the house. Only one, the first I had made out, was facing my way.

Commentary

The symbol here is of horror and corruption at the very 'heart of darkness', evoking a reaction of disgust. The human heads on posts show just how ruthless Kurtz has been, stopping at nothing as he has forced the natives to supply him with ivory. The faces of the severed heads are turned towards the house as though to accuse the person who put them there, but who nevertheless feels no shame in displaying them.

Conrad brings out the force of the symbol through Marlow's physical reaction when he first realises what they are. He recoils 'as if before a blow'. The suggestion that the heads might be eaten by vultures or ants makes the spectacle even more disgusting. The scene is 'ruinous' in a variety of ways, having ultimately destroyed Kurtz as well as his victims.

Symbols such as these can act as a powerful focus for the themes of a narrative, often by providing a concrete object which resonates with all kinds of associations beyond the thing itself. Actions too may be symbolic, often deliberately so, such as the moment when the survivors of the air crash in *Alive* hold a memorial service.

8 More aspects of language: sentences, vocabulary, figurative language and punctuation

Style is both highly personal and infinitely variable. This chapter considers a few of the more obvious aspects of language use you might look out for, but there is no simple formula for analysing style. All we can say in general is that there are many linguistic features that will affect meaning. You will become more aware of these as you consider your set texts in detail through close analysis of the extracts you choose.

Features of language

Sentences

The most obvious thing about sentences is whether they are long or short, but we need to go much further than that in considering the effect of variations. Some long sentences may be highly patterned, others merely rambling. Some short sentences may indicate tension; others may imitate conversational speech patterns.

- Writers may use different sentence lengths and structures to alter the pace of a text.
- Fashions in **syntax**, as in everything else, change over time. There is a strong tendency for old texts to use longer sentences, with more dependent clauses, than modern ones do.

Critical response activity

Two similar descriptive extracts from two of the set texts follow below.

The first is a continuation of Collins's description of Blackwater Park in *The Woman in White*. The second is a descriptive passage taken from Chandler's *The Lady in the Lake*.

- Simply count the number of sentences in the two extracts.
- Identify some of the features of each passage that show change over time.
- Now compare the descriptive elements of the two extracts.

1 Far and near the view suggested the same dreary impressions of solitude and decay, and the glorious brightness of the summer sky overhead seemed only to deepen and harden the gloom and barrenness of the wilderness on which it shone. I turned and retraced my steps to the high heathy ground, directing them a little aside from my former path towards a shabby old wooden shed which stood on the outer skirt of the fir plantation and which had hitherto been too unimportant to share my notice with the wide, wild prospect of the lake.

2 'Back about a mile,' he said, pointing over his shoulder with a thumb, 'there's a little narrow wood road turns over west. You can just drive in and miss the trees. It climbs about five hundred feet in another mile and comes out by Coon Lake. Pretty little place. Folks go up there to picnic once in a while, but not often. It's hard on tyres. There's two three small shallow lakes full of reeds. There's snow up there even now in the shady places.

This chapter covers:

- understanding some effects of sentence structure
- the uses of different kinds of vocabulary
- recognising figurative language
- observing some reasons for variations in punctuation.

AQA Examiner's tip

It is particularly important to avoid feature-spotting when you discuss style – for example, just naming a word as a verb or a sentence as declarative, then moving straight on to discuss something different. What you have to think about all the time is the effect this choice of language has on the meaning of the text.

Key terms

Syntax: the linguistic term for the structure of sentences.

Link

To reread the opening section of Collin's description of Blackwater Park, see page 28.

■ **Further reading**
■ David Crystal, *Rediscover Grammar*, Longman, 2004

■ **Key terms**

Register: a variety of language that is used for particular purposes or within a particular social context. Important features are how formal or how technical the expression is. For example, 'they ain't done nothing' is informal and comes from a spoken register; in a formal written register this is more likely to be 'they have not done anything'. 'A plane' is far less technical than 'a Fairchild F-227'.

Minor sentences: sentences without a verb, most commonly used in conversation.

Complex sentence: a sentence with two or more clauses linked by subordinating conjunctions such as 'which', 'while', 'where'.

Semantic field: a group of words within a text all relating to the same topic.

There's a bunch of old hand-hewn log cabins that's been falling down ever since I recall, and there's a big broken-down frame building that Montclair University used to use for a summer camp maybe years back. They ain't used it in a very long time. This building sits back from the lakes in heavy timber …'

Commentary

Although both extracts describe similar scenes, suitable settings for secrets, this comparison shows different uses of language. In the extract from *The Woman in White*, Marian Halcombe is describing the scene in her diary, so it is presented as a written account. Chandler puts his description into direct speech, giving it to Jim Patton, an old local policeman.

There are some linguistic features that clearly show change over time. Some of this is owing to vocabulary, such as Marian's 'directing' her steps. Some of them occur in the syntax, such as the word order of 'which had hitherto been'. Modern writers are on the whole more sparing of dependent clauses that repeat the relative pronoun 'which', or use it after a preposition, such as 'on which it shone'. These features are not totally archaic – they could occur in modern literature – but they strike us as old-fashioned.

Chandler is aiming for a different kind of realism, in an informal **register**, much closer to the rhythms of everyday speech. He uses **minor sentences** like 'Pretty little place' and colloquial expressions such as 'a bunch of' and 'ain't'.

The two passages also represent a historical change in language use. The first extract has two **complex sentences**, each with dependent clauses; the second slightly longer extract has eleven sentences, two of which are complex.

There has been a considerable change in readers' taste between the dates of publication of the two texts. Modern authors tend not to use such elaborate sentence structures. But Collins was still writing for a wide, popular audience. Many readers in the past liked, and expected, a more elevated style. His descriptions are leisurely here partly because of the method of publication. *The Woman in White* was written to be serialised over many weeks.

Vocabulary

A feature of style that you are bound to notice as you analyse your set texts is the writer's characteristic choice of vocabulary. There are a few particular issues concerning this aspect of language that are worth special attention.

For example, if you look back to the extract from *The Woman in White* above, one of its striking features is the lexical range. A wide variety of words belong to the same **semantic field** of dullness and all reinforce one another. There are the adjectives 'dreary' and 'shabby' and the nouns 'solitude', 'decay', 'gloom', 'barrenness' and 'wilderness'. By contrast, 'glorious brightness' and 'summer' simply reinforce their effect.

Technical language

George Orwell had strong views on vocabulary. In an influential essay called 'Politics and the English Language' he gives a list of rules for good style. Two of them are:

■ Never use a long word where a short one will do.
■ Never use a foreign phrase, a scientific word or a jargon word if you can think of an everyday English equivalent.

This is sound advice for anyone designing a form or writing instructions, and Orwell's own prose is clear, stylish and elegant. However, literary prose is a little more complicated. *The Woman in White* would be a simpler novel if the sentences were shorter and the vocabulary simpler, but it would not necessarily be a better one.

In *The Road to Wigan Pier*, Orwell himself makes clear use of technical vocabulary to give authenticity to his account of the work in coal mines, tactfully explaining the terms as he goes on. For example:

> The statement that a miner receives ten or eleven shillings a shift is very misleading. To begin with, it is only the actual coal 'getter' who is paid at this rate: a 'dataller', for instance, who attends to the roofing, is paid at a lower rate, usually eight or nine shillings a shift.

In *Empire of the Sun* Jim's technical knowledge of Japanese planes, being able to distinguish 'Mitsubishi … Zero-Sen … Nakajima', is an important part of his characterisation, showing a certain, rather surprising, admiration for the Japanese throughout the novel.

Taboo language

Two of the set texts, for different reasons, use language likely to cause offence to some readers. In *The Catcher in the Rye*, Holden Caulfield swears a good deal (though you will notice that he does not use obscenities). Salinger makes him speak very informally in order to create the realistic language of a teenage character. Some people might still object to his speech as blasphemous.

In *The Adventures of Huckleberry Finn* the word commonly used for an African American is 'nigger'. This was normal at the date of publication, but has come to be regarded as deeply offensive. You may, of course, quote from the text, but try to avoid the expression in commentary or creative writing if you can.

Offensive language of any kind is not appropriate for A Level coursework, and you should avoid it in your own work. It may be realistic, but good writers are always conscious of their audience. Your primary audience here consists of your teacher and the AQA moderator, who are more likely to be impressed by literary tact than by **taboo language**.

Archaic vocabulary

When you are comparing one text with another you will sometimes recognise differences owing to linguistic structures or vocabulary that have changed completely over time. It is important to be able to distinguish between words that actually are archaic and words that are simply unfamiliar to you. Here are some examples of words that have dropped out of modern use completely, although you may have met them in your reading of Shakespeare. These are taken from *Robinson Crusoe*:

- ague – fever
- antick – bizarre
- ducats – gold coins
- moiety – half
- succades – sweets.

Wide reading and intelligent use of a dictionary will help you recognise different kinds of vocabulary.

Dictionaries have different purposes. The little ones you can carry around are excellent for checking spelling. For historical meanings you need to consult a larger work that deals with **etymology**.

> ■ **Key terms**
>
> **Taboo language:** language considered offensive or improper to use, and therefore avoided or disapproved of by some speakers.
>
> **Etymology:** the study of the origin and meaning of words.

The *Shorter Oxford English Dictionary* (which is a lot bigger than it sounds from its title) is a good place to look up the history of obscure words. You will probably find it in the reference section of your school or college library. For very rare words, the full 20-volume *Oxford English Dictionary* is available online.

Figurative language

If words have connotations that colour your understanding of a text, so do any comparisons the writer uses. You are probably more aware of the use of **similes** and **metaphors** in poetry than in prose, but all writers use them to some degree.

■ **Critical response activity**

Read this extract from *The Road to Wigan Pier*. List any similes and metaphors you notice in the extract.

What do you think this use of language contributes to the way Orwell represents life in the north of England?

At night, when you cannot see the hideous shapes of houses and the blackness of everything, a town like Sheffield assumes a kind of sinister magnificence. Sometimes the drifts of smoke are rosy with sulphur, and serrated flames, like circular saws, squeeze themselves out from behind the cowls of factory chimneys. Through the open doors of foundries you see fiery serpents of iron being hauled to and fro by redlit boys, and you hear the whizz and bang of steam hammers and the scream of the iron under the blow. The pottery towns are almost equally ugly in a pettier way. Right in amongst the rows of tiny blackened houses, part of the street as it were, are the 'pot banks' – conical brick chimneys like gigantic burgundy bottles buried in the soil and belching their smoke almost in your face. You come upon monstrous clay chasms hundreds of feet deep, with little rusty tubs creeping up on chain railways up one side, and on the other workmen clinging like samphire-gatherers into the face of the cliff with their picks. I passed that way in snowy weather and even the snow was black.

Commentary

This extract is rich in **figurative language**. Similes and metaphors here include:

- flames like circular saws
- fiery serpents of iron
- the scream of the iron
- chimneys like gigantic burgundy bottles
- rusty tubs creeping
- clinging like samphire-gatherers.

In this extract Orwell is stressing the difference between the north and the south of England. He makes the industrial processes of the north seem dangerous but colourful, with comparisons such as 'circular saws' and 'fiery serpents'. The description is full of sense impressions: the red lights, the noise of the hammers, and the smell of sulphur. He **personifies** the industrial process as though it had a life of its own, with expressions such as 'the scream of the iron' and 'tubs creeping'. There is also something strange and even exotic when he compares the shape of the pot-banks to 'burgundy bottles' and the clay workers to 'samphire-gatherers'.

The Road to Wigan Pier is primarily an argument about socialism, but Orwell does not want it to become simply a political tract. To make it readable he includes a good deal of his own experience, both autobiography and description.

Heart of Darkness is particularly full of powerfully evocative imagery. A description of a piece of industrial machinery follows. It has some points of comparison with Orwell's industrial landscape, but also shows how scenes that are in some way similar can have different connotations.

> I came upon a boiler wallowing in the grass, then found a path leading up the hill. It turned aside for the boulders, and also for an undersized railway-truck lying there on its back with its wheels in the air. One was off. The thing looked as dead as the carcass of some animal.

Both these descriptions look at industrial machinery as though it had a life of its own, but whereas Orwell's description is vigorous, Conrad stresses death and decay, even in inanimate objects. The boiler is personified as 'wallowing' as if helpless, and Conrad follows this up even more emphatically with the simile of the truck being 'as dead as the carcass of some animal'. He is suggesting that the rottenness of Africa extends even to the machinery.

In a different context, Raymond Chandler often uses witty and unexpected similes to surprise the reader – for example, 'I separated another dollar from my exhibit and it went into his pocket with a sound like caterpillars fighting' or 'a wizened waiter with evil eyes and a face like a gnawed bone'.

Careful and creative use of figurative language is one quality that distinguishes good writers. It brings description to life by its appeal to the imagination.

Punctuation

In modern times, as well as historical ones, whole books have been written about such matters as punctuation, and you might enjoy one of them, *Eats, Shoots and Leaves* by Lynne Truss, because it is very amusing as well as helpful. It deals with correct uses of punctuation and how this affects meaning. (If you do nothing else, read the panda story on the back cover, which shows exactly how a comma can transform the meaning of a text.)

The purpose of punctuation is to show us how to read a text. It replaces the things that show meaning in oral communication but cannot easily be conveyed in any other way on the printed page: things like where the pauses come, and which words carry emphasis. There are two important points about punctuation.

- In reading older works, including nineteenth-century ones, the text available to you is often not that of the original author but of a later editor. So the line that was printed as 'What! You have no money at the banker's!' in the first edition of *The Woman in White* becomes 'What! You have no money at the bankers?' in the Penguin edition, with a slight but recognisable change of emphasis.

- Punctuation is not so much a stylistic feature in itself, as a way of marking how the text should be read. It is more helpful to observe the rhythms of the writing than to comment on the number of commas or semicolons it uses. Look out for exclamation marks and question marks, which affect the whole tone of a passage, but as with any other feature, ask why they are there and how they affect the overall meaning.

AQA **Examiner's tip**

It is always safest to make positive points about the language of a text and to discuss what is clearly there rather than comment on what is not. If you say that there are no figures of speech you may well be mistaken. Very few texts include no metaphors at all, though it is easy to overlook weaker ones.

Further reading

Lynne Truss, *Eats, Shoots and Leaves*, Profile Books, 2003

Critical response activity

The following extract is from *Robinson Crusoe*, which was originally published in 1719. The original punctuation is very different from modern practice. Read through it and answer the following questions.

■ Can you work out why there are so many capital letters in this sentence?

■ Can you spot any other features that look different from modern punctuation?

> The baking Part was the next Thing to be consider'd, and how I should make Bread when I came to have Corn; for first I had no Yeast; as to that Part, as there was no supplying the Want, so I did not concern myself much about it; But for an Oven, I was indeed in great Pain; at length I found out an Experiment for that also, which was this; I made some Earthen Vessels very broad but not deep; that is to say, about two Foot Diameter, and not above nine inches deep; these I burnt in the Fire, as I had done the other, and laid them by; and when I wanted to bake, I made a great Fire upon my Hearth, which I had pav'd with some square Tiles of my own making, and burning also, but I should not call them square.

Commentary

The capitals are not for emphasis, as you might think; they simply denote nouns. It was normal to write in this way in the eighteenth century, but the practice died out in the nineteenth. Modern editions will normally change the capitals to lowercase letters. A modern editor will also change most of the semicolons to full stops.

Another archaic feature is the use of apostrophes on 'consider'd' and 'pav'd'. These show the pronunciation: the last but one letter, the 'e', has become silent, as we say it now. You probably know from your reading of Shakespeare that very old texts sound the '-ed' ending on words as a separate syllable.

AQA Examiner's tip

Sometimes the style of punctuation shows change over time, and then it may be worth a comment in its own right. Generally, though, you should concentrate on the way punctuation shows meaning in a text.

Students are usually very sensitive to changes over time and quick to spot any cultural references in a book when it mentions details that would be unusual in daily life now. With other kinds of **diachronic variation**, such as vocabulary and grammar, there is a complication because you have to decide whether an expression really has fallen out of use or is just unfamiliar to you personally. You looked at some aspects of this in Chapter 8, and the best help with recognising linguistic change is wide general reading.

Cultural change on a much wider scale can affect the way readers approach texts, especially in matters such as religion, race and the representation of women. In modern literary criticism there has been a great deal of interesting work published on post-colonial literature and on feminist readings.

This chapter covers:

■ observing cultural issues in texts

■ being aware of how cultural change affects criticism.

■ Key terms

Diachronic variation: the changes in language over time.

■ Practical activity

Understanding variations over time is easy. Even if you have not read the books they come from, you can probably have a good guess at which of the following quotations goes furthest back in history, based on your general experience. Put them in chronological order, with the oldest first. What are the most significant clues in each example?

1 It will be seen that the income of a family on the dole normally averages around thirty shillings a week.

2 There was one other thriving business, a shop belonging to a mobile phone company. Like many other cities in Africa, Kisangani had benefited from the communications revolution.

3 Here I stay'd about 20 Days, left them Supplies of all necessary things, and particularly of Arms, Powder, Shot, Cloaths, Tools, and two Workmen, which I brought from *England* with me, *viz.*, a Carpenter and a Smith.

Some cultural issues

Religion

Religion is part of the cultural texture of most pre-twentieth-century literature in a way that may be unfamiliar to modern readers. For example, the early nineteenth century was a time of deep religious controversy. In the early part of the century this was not because of the different explanations of natural phenomena offered by religion and science. Few people questioned the idea that the world was created as the Book of Genesis describes. (Darwin's *On the Origin of Species* was not published until 1859.) There were deep divisions about which group of believers was closest to the central truths of Christianity; the Church of England had fundamental disagreements with both Dissenters and Catholics.

In *North and South* Mr Hale feels compelled to give up his position as a Church of England clergyman because of doubts about doctrine. When Charlotte Brontë read the early chapters, she assumed that this subject was sufficiently important to be the major theme of the novel.

Answers: 3, 1, 2.
3 is *Robinson Crusoe*; the spelling of 'clothes' is odd, and guns no longer use powder. 1 is *The Road to Wigan Pier*; the currency is outdated. 2 is *Blood River*; mobile phones are a recent invention.

Biblical references are common in fiction. Again in *North and South*, Bessy Higgins, who is a young victim of industrial disease, expresses her wish for death by saying, 'I'm weary and tired o' Milton, and longing to get away to the land o' Beulah.'

Critical response activity

Read the following quotation from *North and South*. It is the reply of Bessy to Margaret, the heroine, who tries to comfort her with the hope of heaven.

- Does this response surprise you in any way?
- How do you, the reader, react to it?

'I believe, perhaps more than yo' do o' what's to come. I read the Book o' Revelations until I know it off by heart, and I never doubt when I'm waking, and in my senses, of all the glory I'm to come to.'

Commentary

Bessy is a poorly educated mill hand. She is dying because of all the dust she has inhaled into her lungs. You may find it surprising that in spite of a limited formal education, she reads, and quotes, her Bible constantly. The way you react will depend on your own experience. You may have a strong religious faith yourself and feel a considerable empathy with the viewpoint Bessy represents. On the other hand, a secular audience may find Bessy's piety sentimental rather than uplifting, and need an effort of historical imagination to understand the writer's intentions.

Race

There has been a great deal of interesting critical work recently on what is called 'post-colonial literature'. The term covers a wide variety of texts, including texts set in former colonies and texts by writers whose own background is Indian or African, for example.

As with the issue of religion, modern readers will often bring to a narrative a set of perceptions about race and race relations that are different from those common in its original audience. To take a simple example, Robinson Crusoe names his companion on the island 'Friday' (rather than a usual English forename like Tom, Dick or Harry) and it never seems to occur to him that native islanders have personal names. He automatically assumes that Friday will call him 'Master' and will gratefully consent to be colonised.

Assumptions like this will strike a modern reader as odd. It is important not to get too bogged down in the issue of racial attitudes here, as opposed to other features of the novel, because of its early date. Defoe is reflecting the normal attitudes of his times. But a modern audience, with different cultural attitudes, will read the text differently from the original audience.

Heart of Darkness, Joseph Conrad's novel dating from 1899, is a complex and multi-layered text that has generated a good deal of critical controversy. Tim Butcher writes that in his schooldays: 'My friends and I would argue about whether Conrad was being racist, suggesting that black Africa was in some way inherently evil, or whether he used equatorial Africa simply as a backdrop for a novel about how wicked any human can become.'

Critical response activity

In the following extract from *Heart of Darkness*, Conrad makes clear that Kurtz and the colonial company that employs him are undoubtedly corrupt.

How does the language here suggest the complexities of Conrad's attitude?

I had to look after the savage who was fireman. He was an improved specimen; he could fire up a vertical boiler. He was there below me, and, upon my word, to look at him was as edifying as seeing a dog in a parody of breeches and a feather hat, walking on his hind legs. A few months of training had done for that really fine chap. He squinted at the steam-gauge and at the water-gauge with an evident effort of intrepidity – and he had filed teeth too, the poor devil, and the wool of his pate shaved into queer patterns, and three ornamental scars on each of his cheeks. He ought to have been clapping his hands and stamping his feet on the bank, instead of which he was hard at work, a thrall to strange witchcraft, full of improving knowledge.

Commentary

There is an unmistakeable note of sarcasm in the phrase 'improving knowledge'. The white colonists have not brought improvement to Africa, merely pillaged it. The passage is ambivalent, however. The phrase 'really fine chap' might express admiration, but the word 'specimen' and the comparison with 'a dog in a parody of breeches and a feather hat' appear contemptuous. The white traders have abused the natives in the way they have been employed, and are rightly condemned, but the suggestion that the fireman is inherently too primitive to learn about engines is disturbing.

Feminism

Over the last fifty years feminist writers have done some of the most interesting work in literary criticism and have approached texts in new and striking ways. *Testament of Youth* is particularly interesting in its author's approach to feminism.

Critical response activity

Consider this extract from *Testament of Youth*. It comes from a letter Vera Brittain wrote to her future husband. What do you see as Brittain's dominant attitude in her approach to marriage?

'For me … the feminist problem ranks with your economic problem. Just as you want to discover how a man can maintain a decent standard of culture on a small income, so I want to solve the problem of how a married woman, without being inordinately rich, can have children and yet maintain her intellectual and spiritual independence as well as having … time for the pursuit of her own career. For the unmarried woman there is now no problem provided that she has the will to work. For a married woman without children there is only a psychological problem – a problem of prejudice – which can be overcome by determination. But the other problem – that of the woman with children – remains the most vital.'

Commentary

The word 'problem' occurs six times in this extract. She carefully lists different possibilities using a sharply intellectual approach.

Attitudes have changed only slowly, however. George Orwell, writing in 1937, four years after Vera Brittain's book came out, commented:

> In a working-class home it is the man who is the master and not, as in a middle-class home, the woman or the baby. Practically never, for instance, in a working-class home, will you see the man doing a stroke of housework.

This is not just a historical subject. The representation of women in literature and in literary non-fiction remains an important area for study.

Think about it

In creative writing, what effect on different plot lines has been brought about by:

■ Trains and the motor car replacing horses?

■ The invention of aeroplanes?

■ The development of automatic weapons?

■ The invention of the mobile telephone?

Practical activity

List the female characters in the two texts you have been studying and consider how much they initiate the action and how much they are passive or minor characters.

Is there any significant difference between the older and the more modern text?

10 Research and readership: themes in their context

Texts do not exist in isolation. They are influenced by the period in which they were written, and in turn readers interpret them according to their own experience and cultural attitudes. You will understand the texts you are studying better if you know something about their background, and this involves doing some research.

Background research

Before you get very far with your coursework you will find it helpful to have some background information about the texts you are studying and the conditions under which they were produced. How should you go about this?

You will find the huge variety of resources available on the internet invaluable. For example, *Blood River* has an excellent website at www.bloodriver.co.uk. Think carefully about your organisation, however. Log on to a search engine and simply type in 'Robinson Crusoe': you will get more than 8,000 entries. Because of the way search engines operate, the most useful web pages are likely to be towards the head of the list, but not necessarily, and the various articles available will vary from scholarly studies to unreliable and eccentric articles.

Different key words will produce different results. In order to get the best out of search engines, you have to think first what kind of information you really want. It might be:

- background about the author's life
- other works by the same author for comparison
- critical studies
- works used or referred to in the set text
- historical details concerning the narrative's setting.

At some point you are probably going to use Wikipedia, which is one of the most exciting research tools, but be cautious. Anyone can write the articles, and though many of them are excellent, many also contain mistakes. You need to double-check information you find on the internet.

Websites come and go at speed. When you use an internet site you should record not only the web address but also the date on which you last accessed it, as your evidence of research.

Do not neglect books. It may seem obvious, but it is easy to overlook what is right in front of you.

- The text you are studying will usually tell you when it was first published, on the imprint page.
- Read the introduction, if there is one. Sometimes there is useful material, such as a chronology of the author's life, or some historical background, and this will have been checked by the editor and is likely to be reliable. There may be several editions of classic texts available at the same time in a good bookshop. If the first edition you see does not have notes and an introduction, check whether there are others that do.

This chapter covers:

- researching into the background of your texts using reference sources
- being aware of readership
- different kinds of background information
- the relevance of a writer's biography.

AQA Examiner's tip

Coursework involves many different kinds of activity. The point about background research is that it can improve your understanding of the set texts. If you have spent a lot of time finding out about background, you can rightly be proud of it, but you have to process it in your head and use it in the right way. Do not copy background notes directly into your analysis of extracts. Your research will show up through your greater understanding of the texts themselves.

Your school or college library will almost certainly have a reference section that will help you find basic facts. Here are some standard works that you might find useful.

■ *The Oxford Companion to English Literature*, ed. Margaret Drabble, 6th edition, 2000

■ *The Cambridge Guide to Literature in English*, ed. Dominic Head, 2006

■ *Chambers Biographical Dictionary*, ed. Chambers and Joan Bakewell, 2011

Historical audiences

It is helpful to consider what the original audience of a text was like, and what its expectations were. There are some common oversimplifications here that you need to avoid. If you go back far enough in time, it is true that books were a rarity and educated audiences relatively small. By the nineteenth century things had altogether changed, however. Cheap machine printing came in around 1840, and for the rest of the century, literacy increased fast, and so did the appetite for newspapers and books as a form of entertainment.

Literacy and circulation figures

By the nineteenth century there were many schools, even for the poor, although they were of very variable quality. The Sunday schools, among others, made a great contribution. There were still people who were illiterate (there still are today), but by the middle of the nineteenth century about three-quarters of the population probably had some reading ability. If you think about it, there are many trades where literacy is essential, and in an age when all business documents were written out by hand, huge numbers of people were employed as clerks. Servants in a big country house would often be allowed to use the library there. Gabriel Betteredge, the comic old house steward in Collins's novel *The Moonstone* (1868), uses *Robinson Crusoe* rather like a Bible. He tells us:

> I have worn out six stout *Robinson Crusoes* with hard work in my service. On my lady's last birthday she gave me a seventh. I took a drop too much on the strength of it; and *Robinson Crusoe* put me right again. Price four shillings and sixpence, bound in blue, with a picture into the bargain.

Circulation figures could be large, even by modern standards. In 1850, when the population was approximately 18 million, the first number of Dickens's *Household Words* cost twopence and sold 100,000 copies. (This periodical is where a large number of Victorian novels were published for the first time as serials, including *North and South*.) After a time, *Household Words* settled down to a rather lower circulation figure of 38,500 a week; a less literary penny weekly, the *Family Herald*, was selling 300,000 copies a week in 1854. In the US, *Uncle Tom's Cabin*, by Harriet Beecher Stowe (1852), is credited as the first novel to sell a million copies.

One common mistake is to think of reading as an 'upper-class' activity in the nineteenth century. This is to misunderstand the nature of Victorian society. In 1844, Lord Jeffrey wrote an essay on the poet Crabbe (published in *Contributions to the Edinburgh Review*). He said, 'In this country there probably are not less than three hundred thousand persons who read for instruction and amusement among the middling classes of society. In the higher classes there are not as many as thirty thousand.' All this is relevant to your understanding of those set texts that were written in the nineteenth century, and the audience their authors expected.

Think about it

In both the eighteenth and nineteenth centuries it was common for families to read aloud to each other as a form of entertainment. What influence might this development have had on the choice of subjects and on styles of writing?

Intertextuality

You will remember that Holden Caulfield uses 'that David Copperfield kind of stuff' as a shorthand expression for giving biographical information at the beginning of a story. Salinger assumes that the reader will know that this refers to a novel by Charles Dickens.

It may be helpful to know what other books or literary traditions the original audience is likely to have been familiar with. **Intertextuality** is important for some narratives. Tom Sawyer has done a great deal of reading about the correct way to arrange for the escape of prisoners and reproaches Huck for his ignorance: 'Why, hain't you ever read any books at all – Baron Trenck, nor Casanova, nor Benvenuto Chelleeny, nor Henri IV, nor none of them heroes?' The full comic flavour of his adventures comes out if you are able to compare the imprisonment of Jim with some knowledge of *The Count of Monte Cristo*.

Marlow's journey up the Congo in *Heart of Darkness* is compared to Dante's descent into the circles of hell in the *Inferno*. In a different context, *Testament of Youth* makes use of the same image:

> For nearly a month the camp resembled a Gustave Doré illustration to Dante's *Inferno*. Sisters flying from the captured Casualty Clearing Stations crowded into our quarters; often completely without belongings, they took possession of our rooms, our beds, and all our spare uniforms.

In its turn *Blood River* makes a number of explicit references to *Heart of Darkness* that contribute to the tone of Butcher's account. Here is one where he borrows and develops an image from *Heart of Darkness* to describe the landscape.

> Conrad likened the river to a serpent coiling right across Africa. In these upper reaches the snake was fat and lifeless.

Practical activity

You could make a list of any books or periodicals referred to in your set text, including such works as the Bible. This often gives an insight into the author's attitudes and values.

The relevance of the author's life and times

Biographical information about the author of your set text will probably to be one of the first things you look for, and this will almost certainly be interesting. People who write autobiographies are likely to be those who have lived through extraordinary circumstances. Writers of fiction have often led colourful lives. But think carefully before you put too much of this into the first part of your coursework, taking up valuable space: how relevant is it to the extracts you choose?

Authenticity of experience, however, makes a great deal of difference. Both Joseph Conrad and Mark Twain worked on river boats, and you can see that their practical experience in real life gives them technical knowledge about navigation that they use in their fiction.

Critical response activity

Heart of Darkness never explicitly calls the river the Congo, but the voyage is convincing. Read this short extract from the novel. How does Conrad make Marlow's experience realistic here?

Key terms

Intertextuality: the way one text partly depends for its meaning on reference to another text.

Think about it

Are these facts likely to be of any real use in your coursework, or should you discard them as irrelevancies?

- Wilkie Collins was a drug addict.
- Daniel Defoe wrote *Robinson Crusoe* at the age of nearly 60.
- In later life, J. D. Salinger became a recluse.

I had to mess about with white-lead and strips of woollen blanket, helping to put bandages on those leaky steam-pipes – I tell you I had to watch the steering, and circumvent those snags, and get the tin-pot along by hook or by crook.

Commentary

There is a sense not only of the narrator being harrassed by the number of tasks all needing attention at once, but also of those tasks being precisely listed by someone who has experience of the situation. He does not just say 'repairs' to the steam-pipes, but tells us exactly how he dealt with the problem, with 'white-lead and strips of woollen blanket', while steering so as to avoid hazards in the water itself. Conrad wants us to believe in Marlow as a narrator because he needs to give credibility to the violence and horror at the end of the story. Using his own experience helps him to do this.

In *Empire of the Sun* J. G. Ballard draws on actual childhood experience of life in a Japanese prison camp at Lunghua, where he was interned from 1942 (when he was aged 12) to the end of the war in 1945. Elizabeth Gaskell was the wife of a Unitarian minister and lived in Manchester. (You can still see her old house there.)

All these writers successfully use what they know about in real life to make their fiction credible, and this is important. But remember that what you are discussing in your coursework is what each of them actually wrote and how they crafted their material, wherever it came from.

AQA Examiner's tip

The space you are allowed in your coursework is valuable. Use it to show your skills in analysis of the extracts you have chosen from your set texts, backed up by a brief mention of biographical or historical background where this is relevant.

Some features of context summarised

Text	Date	Setting	Context
Robinson Crusoe	1719	Caribbean	Based on the experiences of Alexander Selkirk marooned 1704–9
North and South	1855	Victorian England (Manchester)	Mrs Gaskell was married to a Unitarian minister living in Manchester
The Woman in White	1860	Victorian England	Legal background on inheritance is of interest
The Adventures of Huckleberry Finn	1884	Mississippi River, USA	American Civil War 1861–5 was fought on the issue of the abolition of slavery
Heart of Darkness	1899	Not named, but recognisably the Congo	Belgian colony under Leopold II
Testament of Youth	1933	Buxton, Oxford, London, Malta, France	First World War 1914–18 Women over the age of 30 allowed to vote 1918 League of Nations founded 1919
The Road to Wigan Pier	1937	North of England, especially mining areas	Depression of the 1930s
The Lady in the Lake	1943	California, USA	Second World War 1939–45
The Catcher in the Rye	1951	New York, USA	
Alive	1974	Andes Mountains, actually Argentina, but potential rescuers thought the accident occurred in Chile	Rugby team from Catholic college in Uruguay Plane crash took place 12 October 1972
Empire of the Sun	1984	Shanghai, China Lunghua internment camp	Second World War 1939–45
Blood River	2006	River Congo	Expedition 2004 retraced the journey of H. M. Stanley 1874–7

How should this coursework assignment be planned and completed? Careful planning right from the beginning will save you a lot of trouble later on. You need to keep a record in your notes of everything you do and when, so that you can provide evidence of planning when you submit your final coursework.

Choosing the extracts for your analysis

- First of all, read the whole of both books through quickly, before you start studying them in depth. This will give you an idea of the plot and the main features of each book as a whole.

- Read both books again carefully in the light of your given theme.

- Choose extracts of 500 to 800 words from each book that are reasonably self-contained to work on. Do not exceed the word limit.

- Look for passages that have some similarities of subject matter and make similar contributions to the structure of the novel as a whole.

- Choose passages that will give you the opportunity to discuss in detail some of the features of writing that we have discussed earlier in this book, such as methods of characterisation, setting or imagery.

- Remember that you need to give approximately equal space in your analysis to each of the two extracts.

- You should submit your two extracts as photocopies of the text, clearly marked 'Start' and 'Finish'. Do not retype them.

Writing your coursework

When you do the actual writing:

- Some comparison of the two texts is required. It is a good idea to explain in the beginning what the links are between them and how they both fit the theme. However, you do not need to mention both texts in every paragraph. Sometimes it is more effective to deal with points from each in turn.

- Bear in mind the word limit throughout. Your analysis should be 1,200 to 1,500 words long. You should produce a first draft and then improve it as necessary to produce a final draft for submission. You are not required to submit earlier drafts.

- Few writers do everything perfectly at their first attempt. Some redrafting is a normal part of preparing your work for assessment. You should produce a first draft and then improve it as necessary to produce a final draft for submission. You are not required to submit earlier drafts.

- Leave some time between writing the first draft and correcting it. It is much easier to see mistakes and potential improvements after an interval of rest. The spellcheck is a great help and you should always use it, but be careful and do not rely on it entirely. For example, it will not pick up mistakes such as writing 'there' instead of 'their'.

This chapter covers:

- drawing on insights from literary and linguistic studies in long-term planning

- choosing suitable text extracts

- understanding assessment criteria.

AQA Examiner's tip

Allow yourself plenty of time to work on your coursework, especially as the deadline approaches. It is a good idea to leave longer than you believe you will actually need, to allow for the possibility of accidents such as being ill or your printer breaking down. Coursework that is rushed for submission at the last minute is unlikely to do you justice.

A worked example of full-length analytical coursework

Here are some ideas about theme, style and change over time, put together in a single example.

Suppose your set texts are *The Woman in White* and *The Lady in the Lake*, and your set theme is suspense. A number of passages would do very well to illustrate this. The two extracts chosen below have strong similarities as well as differences. Each builds up to a moment when the narrator is about to make a discovery.

Extract A: The Woman in White

I placed myself sideways against the railing of the verandah – first ascertaining by touching them the position of the flowerpots on either side of me. There was room enough for me to sit between them and no more. The sweet-scented leaves of the flower on my left hand just brushed my cheek as I lightly rested my head against the railing.

The first sounds that reached me from below were caused by the opening or closing (most probably the latter) of three doors in succession – the doors, no doubt, leading into the hall and into the rooms on each side of the library, which the Count had pledged himself to examine. The first object that I saw was the red spark again travelling out into the night from under the verandah, moving away towards my window, waiting a moment, and then returning to the place from which it had set out.

'The devil take your restlessness! When do you mean to sit down?' growled Sir Percival's voice beneath me.

'Ouf! How hot it is!' said the Count, sighing and puffing wearily.

His exclamation was followed by the scraping of the garden chairs on the tiled pavement under the verandah – the welcome sound which told me they were going to sit close to the window as usual. So far the chance was mine. The clock in the turret struck the quarter to twelve as they settled themselves in their chairs. I heard Madame Fosco through the open window yawning, and saw her shadow pass once more across the white face of the blind.

Meanwhile, Sir Percival and the Count began talking together below, now and then dropping their voices a little lower than usual, but never sinking them to a whisper. The strangeness and peril of my situation, the dread, which I could not master, of Madame Fosco's lighted window, made it difficult, almost impossible, for me, at first, to keep my presence of mind, and to fix my attention solely on the conversation beneath. For some minutes I could only succeed in gathering the general substance of it. I understood the Count to say that the one window alight was his wife's, that the ground floor of the house was quite clear, and that they might now speak to each other without fear of accidents. Sir Percival merely answered by upbraiding his friend with having unjustifiably slighted his wishes and neglected his interests all through the day. The Count thereupon defended himself by declaring that he had been beset by certain troubles and anxieties which had absorbed all his attention, and that the only safe time to come to an explanation was a time when they could feel certain of being neither interrupted nor overheard. 'We are at a serious crisis in our affairs, Percival,' he said, 'and if we are to decide the future at all, we must decide secretly tonight.'

That sentence of the Count's was the first which my attention was ready enough to master exactly as it was spoken. From this point, with certain breaks and interruptions, my whole interest fixed breathlessly on the conversation, and I followed it word for word.

'Crisis?' repeated Sir Percival. 'It's a worse crisis than you think for, I can tell you.'

'So I should suppose from your behaviour for the last day or two,' returned the other coolly. 'But wait a little. Before we advance to what I do not know, let us be quite certain of what I do know. Let us first see if I am right about the time that is past, before I make any proposal for the time that is to come.'

'Stop till I get the brandy and water. Have some yourself.'

'Thank you, Percival. The cold water with pleasure, a spoon, and the basin of sugar. Eau sucrée, my friend – nothing more.'

'Sugar-and-water for a man of your age! – There! mix your sickly mess. You foreigners are all alike.'

'Now listen, Percival. I will put our position plainly before you, as I understand it, and you shall say if I am right or wrong. You and I both came back to this house from the Continent with our affairs seriously embarrassed.'

'Cut it short! I wanted some thousands and you some hundreds, and without the money we were both in a fair way to go to the dogs together. There's the situation. Make what you can of it. Go on.'

(738 words)

Extract B: The Lady in the Lake

Half an hour passed. Without tobacco it seemed a long time. Then far off I heard a car motor start up and grow louder and the white beam of headlights passed below me on the road. The sound faded into the distance and a faint dry tang of dust hung in the air for a while after it was gone.

I got out of my car and walked back to the gate and to the Chess cabin. A hard push opened the sprung window this time. I climbed in again and let myself down to the floor and poked the flash I had brought across the room to the table lamp. I switched the lamp on and listened a moment, heard nothing and went out to the kitchen. I switched on a hanging bulb over the sink.

The wood-box beside the stove was neatly piled with split wood. There were no dirty dishes in the sink, no foul-smelling pots on the stove. Bill Chess, lonely or not, kept his house in good order. A door opened from the kitchen into the bedroom, and from that a very narrow door led into a tiny bathroom which had evidently been built on to the cabin fairly recently. The clean celotex lining showed that. The bathroom told me nothing.

The bedroom contained a double bed, a pinewood dresser with a round mirror on the wall above it, a bureau, two straight chairs and a tin waste-basket. There were two oval rag rugs on the floor, one on each side of the bed. On the walls Bill Chess had tacked up a set of war maps from the *National Geographic*. There was a silly-looking red-and-white flounce on the dressing table.

I poked around in the drawers. An imitation leather trinket-box with an assortment of gaudy costume jewellery had not been taken away. There was the usual stuff women use on their faces and finger-nails and eyebrows, and it seemed to me that there was too much of it. But that was just guessing. The bureau contained both man's and woman's clothes, not a great deal of either. Bill Chess had a very noisy check shirt with starched matching collar, among other things. Underneath a sheet of blue tissue paper in one corner I found something I didn't like. A seemingly brand-new peach-coloured slip trimmed with lace. Silk slips were not being left behind that year, not by any woman in her senses.

This looked bad for Bill Chess. I wondered what Patton had thought of it.

I went back to the kitchen and prowled the open shelves above and beside the sink. They were thick with cans and jars of household staples. The confectioner's sugar was in a square brown box with a torn corner. Patton had made an attempt to clean up what was spilled. Near the sugar were salt, borax, baking-soda, cornstarch, brown sugar and so on. Something might be hidden in any of them.

Something that had been clipped from a chain anklet whose cut ends did not fit together.

I shut my eyes and poked a finger at random and it came to rest on the baking-soda. I got a newspaper from the back of the wood-box and spread it out and dumped the soda out of the box. I stirred it around with a spoon. There seemed to be an indecent lot of baking-soda, but that was all there was. I funnelled it back into the box and tried the borax. Nothing but borax. Third time lucky. I tried the cornstarch. It made too much fine dust, and there was nothing but cornstarch.

The sound of distant steps froze me to the ankles. I reached up and yanked the light out and dodged back into the living room and reached for the lamp switch. Much too late to be of any use of course. The steps sounded again, soft and cautious. The hackles rose on my neck.

I waited in the dark, with the flash in my left hand. A deadly long two minutes crept by. I spent some of the time breathing, but not all.

It wouldn't be Patton. He would walk up to the door and open it and tell me off. The careful quiet steps seemed to move this way and that, a movement, a long pause, another movement, another long pause. I sneaked across to the door and twisted the knob silently. I yanked the door wide and stabbed out with the flash.

It made golden lamps of a pair of eyes. There was a leaping movement and a quick thudding of hoofs back among the trees. It was only an inquisitive deer.

(778 words)

Sample response

Suspense is an important element in the structure of both these novels; information emerges gradually in the course of the plot, leading stage by stage to the solution of a central mystery. Here each narrator is on the verge of making a significant discovery. The reader is kept waiting for the moment when a clue will be revealed. Both these extracts are first-person narratives, so an important element of suspense occurs because both narrators are hiding and in danger of discovery themselves. They each take risks as they try to find out the truth, and we share their anxiety. Both scenes in these extracts take place in darkness. In each of them it is the middle of the night, and the darkness is symbolic of hidden secrets.

> Overview with link to theme of suspense

> Notes point of view of narrator and how this affects the theme

> Identifies symbolism as another layer of meaning

In *The Woman in White*, Marian Halcombe hides on the roof of a verandah while she discovers details of the 'crisis' in Percival Glyde's financial affairs. Percival is desperate to get access to his wife's money. In the passage following this extract, Marian is about to hear that Count Fosco would not stop at murder to obtain her sister Laura's fortune. In *The Lady in the Lake*, Philip Marlowe is hiding so that he can investigate the contents of Bill Chess's cabin in secret. (At this stage in the novel it seems possible that Chess has murdered his wife.) Marlowe is about to discover an important clue to the identity of one of the two missing women. Chandler creates suspense as Marlowe searches for a missing anklet. When he finds it, immediately after this extract, he discovers that Chess's wife was living under a false name.

> Sets extracts briefly in the context of the plot

> Contextualises the action

Collins builds up the atmosphere carefully, holding back the information about Percival's debts for a while, and focusing on Marian's position as eavesdropper. He emphasises her courage and resourcefulness, two of the dominant characteristics he gives her throughout the novel. Marian's position is extremely precarious, perched on a narrow ledge, in danger of betraying her position by knocking over a flowerpot, or of being discovered by Madame Fosco, who is just the other side of a window. We follow the experience in detail through her sensations. The description of the scene is full of precise sense impressions, which make it convincing as well as tense: the 'sweet-scented' leaves of the flower beside Marian; the heat of the night; the incidental sounds of the 'scraping of the garden chairs on the tiled pavement' and the clock striking; the sight of the 'red spark' of Fosco's cigar as he moves around.

> Observes writer's technique of withholding information

> Notes the effect of descriptive detail and the contribution of sense impressions

The narrative at first summarises the beginning of the conversation between the two men, setting the context with a general explanation of why this discussion between them has been left so late in the day. Ironically this is a time when Fosco feels safe from being overheard. Then Collins uses direct speech to make the main substance of the conversation more dramatic, beginning with Fosco's statement that 'if we are to decide the future at all, we must decide secretly tonight'. This immediately rivets Marian's attention; so does Fosco's declaration to Percival that he is about to 'put our position plainly before you'. The use of speech signals strongly that an important revelation is about to take place.

> Irony of the context explained; a comment on the setting

> The purpose and effect of the writer's use of direct speech explained

Collins keeps the suspense going a little longer, even at this point, delaying the action while the men settle down with drinks. He adds distinctive touches to the characterisation of each. Percival is surly and ill-tempered, speaking in abrupt sentences like 'Cut it short!' Fosco is a different kind of villain altogether. His habit of drinking nothing

> Brief comments on character develop the contrast between the two villains

but sugar-water, like a child, and his smooth talk make him even more sinister. The characters are contrasted, but both are evidently dangerous as they talk about the lengths they are prepared to go to for money.

Chandler, too, allows time to elapse while Marlowe waits to be sure that he is alone and that the policeman, Joe Patton, is well clear of the scene. The apparently trivial discovery Patton made of a broken anklet chain in the Chess cabin has set Marlowe thinking. He follows through a line of reasoning with characteristic logic, and is not to be put off. Like Marian Halcombe, he is resourceful in creating an opportunity to make discoveries.

The description of the tidy cabin takes up a good deal of space because of its detail, listing furniture and clothes in a way that tells us the detective is missing nothing. His reasoning is deductive – for example he knows that the bathroom is new because 'The clean celotex lining showed that'. By this stage in the novel, the reader is well aware of Marlowe's methods. We know that when he observes small things they are likely to be significant. The silk petticoat left in a drawer suggests to Marlowe that perhaps Bill Chess did kill his wife, as she would be unlikely to leave something so desirable behind if she ran away. The possibility remains as one of a number of explanations until later in the novel.

Patton found the broken chain by accident. Marlowe searches for its missing part systematically. Suspense builds here as his narrative takes us through the boxes of white powder in the kitchen one at a time, finding nothing. When he hears steps outside, we expect that he is about to confront an intruder, although it turns out to be just a deer. Chandler creates tension through Marlowe's reactions in such phrases as 'froze me to the ankles', 'yanked the light out', and 'The hackles rose on my neck', then follows this by a comic anticlimax as the animal appears. He finds the identity disk hidden in the box of icing sugar only after all this delay. It reveals that Chess's wife was living under an assumed name and has a suspicious past.

Although these are both first-person narratives they are presented differently. Marian Halcombe is writing in her diary, and her prose is more formal than Philip Marlowe's account. It is also characteristic of the date of *The Woman in White* that the narrator should use a higher proportion of complex sentences than is common in modern prose. The sentence beginning 'The first sounds that reached me from below …' for example, has multiple subordinate clauses and definitely belongs to the register of written language. Phrases such as 'most probably the latter' and 'pledged himself to examine' have a literary flavour. There is a noticeable difference between this and the direct speech in the extract.

The whole of Marlowe's narrative is much closer to the rhythms of speech, containing a far higher proportion of simple or compound sentences and colloquial phrases such as 'Third time lucky'. It contains no conversation, for the obvious reason that Marlowe is completely alone, but it still sounds like his speaking voice, and it has a faster pace than Marian's narrative in spite of elaborating on the search of the cabin to maintain suspense. The verbs Chandler uses to describe action are strong and vigorous – 'yanked' (twice), 'dodged', 'twisted' and 'stabbed'. His characteristic habit of using humorous turns of phrase in dangerous situations comes through in the sentence 'I spent some of the time breathing, but not all.'

Marginal annotations:

Link to second text through comparison of situation

Link to second text through comparison of character

Mentions listing as a descriptive technique, and its purpose

Gives a characteristic example of the detective's methods

Explains the significance of a possible clue in the plot

Further links to the theme of suspense, and comments on the creation of atmosphere

Comparison of linguistic features: notes the differences in register between the two extracts, with a comment relating this to change over time

Appropriate use of technical terminology to explore meaning

Notes an example of humour related to the writer's distinctive witty style

Although the plot of both these novels turns on the fact of one woman being mistaken for another, the time gap between them shows in all kinds of differences. Modern villains are more likely to be ordinary policemen than members of the aristocracy like Sir Percival Glyde. Crime, it seems, has become more democratic over the years. Laura Fairlie is in danger because complex property laws mean that her husband wants the right to control her money and she has little freedom of action. The position of women has changed beyond recognition since Victorian times. Count Fosco refers to his favourite sugar water as 'eau sucrée'. The choice of a foreign word seems as unlikely as the choice of drink in a modern context.

Explores contextual features showing change over time

The language of *The Woman in White* contains subtle differences from modern usage. While expressions such as Sir Percival's 'upbraiding his friend with having unjustifiably slighted his wishes' are not absolutely archaic, the language appears over-elaborate to a modern ear, using a long word where a short one would do. The language of *The Lady in the Lake* contains examples of distinctively American usage, such as 'confectioner's sugar' (where British English uses 'icing sugar'), or 'bureau' as a piece of furniture to store clothes. However, none of these appears dated as in the earlier of the two novels.

Explores linguistic features of change over time and notes differences between British and American usage

Raymond Chandler's novel is simpler than Wilkie Collins's in language and in structure. Collins has a multi-layered approach, using different narrators in sequence to reveal aspects of the plot, whereas Chandler makes Marlowe reveal all the information himself as he pieces it together. Both rely equally on suspense, however, withholding information from the reader and revealing it only gradually, to maintain interest.

Brief summing up to conclude the comparison

(1,495 words)

Commentary

This answer is not perfect, but it should achieve a very good pass. It fulfils most of the assessment criteria, and keeps in the foreground the set theme of suspense. It uses brief illustrative quotations, while keeping within the word limit for both extracts and analysis. The extracts are carefully chosen to give a number of points of comparison in both situation and language. There is a balance between the two of them; neither text dominates unduly.

Although it shows awareness of the way these extracts fit into the wider context of the two novels, this answer does not use up a great deal of the space available on general background or telling the story. It concentrates on actual analysis, using relevant approaches from integrated linguistic literary study and appropriate critical terminology (Assessment Objective 1).

A good script will show knowledge and understanding of the theme and be able to set the chosen extracts in the context of the whole work. This answer draws attention to the extracts' contribution to the plot. It also shows some knowledge of the wider context in which the two books were written, although within the word limit there is not much space to elaborate on this.

The coursework should show understanding of such matters as genre, characterisation and tone. Here there is awareness that although *The Woman in White* is not a detective story like *The Lady in the Lake*, it works on the gradual unravelling of a mystery. There is some comment on the way character is developed in each text.

Responses to literary texts should also show understanding of narrative methods such as establishing a point of view and the use of dialogue. The script above explores the use of first-person narratives and their effect, differentiating between the two texts and relating this to change over time. It picks up on the use of sense impressions and the relevance of close detail in description.

Linguistic features are important in an integrated approach. The script should show understanding of how form, style and vocabulary shape meaning. Here the answer makes a contrast between the relative formality of the Collins extract and Chandler's more colloquial style. A good script should always use the technical vocabulary of criticism, not just to identify textual features but to show how they bring out meaning, as this one does. 'Feature spotting' is unhelpful because it does not in itself explain, or develop, a coherent analysis.

Finally, coursework needs to pay careful attention to presentation. To gain high marks, the analysis has to show a command of written expression that is both accurate and coherent.

The creative task

This part of your coursework asks you to undertake a realistic exercise. All successful writers learn from one another; professional writers do so just as much as A Level students. Throughout this unit you have been thinking about writing techniques as you have studied the set texts. Now it is time for you to put some of your ideas into practice with a short piece of creative writing of your own. The limit for this is 500 to 850 words, which represents about two sides of typed A4 paper, depending on point size and layout. You may find that you have soon used up the word limit and you want to write more. You must resist that temptation and concentrate instead on producing focused and controlled writing that displays your skills within this 500- to 850-word frame.

This unit covers:

- the requirements for creative writing coursework

- the relationship between creative writing and your set texts.

Approaching creative writing

This section of the book, on creative writing, concentrates on choices of point of view, genre and audience, which are all features you have already considered in relation to other authors' work. It makes further practical suggestions on how to adapt these in your own writing as you develop your own ideas and style. In Chapter 15 you will find examples of creative coursework with examiners' comments to help you judge how to develop your writing skills and so gain good marks.

You are likely to complete the creative writing task at a fairly late stage in your course, when you have a thorough knowledge of the set texts, but do not leave all the planning till the end, hoping for sudden inspiration. It is always better to have something to reject or adapt rather than facing a completely blank page, even though you may well come to discard many of your early ideas in favour of others. Professional writers tend to keep a notebook handy, where they jot down ideas and phrases they may want to use later.

Your aim is to surprise and delight your reader by original work that somehow enriches their idea of the original text. You do not have to agree with the point of view expressed or implied in the set texts themselves; you may challenge it if you wish. As you have already learned, context is important, and attitudes that seem obvious to one group of readers may seem very strange to another. To see this, you have only to think of how in the last century attitudes to race, the position of women, and even something as commonplace as smoking have changed.

This creative writing coursework is a test of your:

- understanding of one or both of the texts
- understanding of the theme you have been studying
- knowledge of different genres and their conventions

- ability to interest an audience
- own command of English
- ability to control your writing to meet a specific word limit. (This will be strictly enforced.)

The basic information in this part of your coursework *must* come from the set books themselves. You might, for example, choose to adopt the point of view of a minor character. You might adapt the material for a different audience or a different genre. You could even combine the two set texts by creating an imaginary situation where a character from one book meets a character from another. But simply writing a new text in the same genre – for example, travel writing – without detailed reference to the original set text will not fulfil your brief.

12 Challenging the point of view

There is always more than one side to a story. Courts of law, for example, acknowledge this in real life; they listen to the case for both sides, the prosecution and defence, and make a judgment between them.

When we discussed point of view in Chapter 3, we noted that one of the features of a first-person narrative is possible bias. This is not necessarily a disadvantage. Writers may use different points of view creatively, either in different narratives or within different parts of the same one. You may have read Shelley's *Frankenstein*, where Victor Frankenstein and the Creature give totally different accounts of the Creature's first moments, and the reader has to choose between them. Or you may know Golding's *Lord of the Flies*, which was written in reaction to Ballantyne's *Coral Island*. Ballantyne's Jack, Ralph and Peterkin have fun and show strength of character when marooned on a desert island, but Golding's schoolboys degenerate into savages.

Here is an example of one character's very biased account, taken from one of the set texts.

In *The Woman in White*, Wilkie Collins uses multiple narrators, all with their own points of view. Count Fosco is a villain, intelligent, ruthless and completely unscrupulous. Towards the end of the novel, Collins gives Fosco a narrative of his own. Collins himself clearly does not approve of Fosco's morals (or lack of them) any more than his hero and other main characters do, and the text challenges the reader to make a judgement.

The essential part of the plot is this: Anne Catherick and Laura Fairlie (Lady Glyde) are remarkably similar in appearance. In order to get Laura's money, Fosco imprisons her in an asylum, pretending that she is Anne, who is mentally deranged. Anne dies and is buried under a tombstone with Laura's name on it.

This chapter covers:

- exploring possible relationships between narratives

- understanding what is meant by challenging a point of view

- seeing how one text, or part of a text, may depend on another and yet differ from it.

Critical response activity

Read the following extract from *The Woman in White*.

- What is the case for the prosecution here?
- What is Fosco's defence?
- How does he try to convince us of his own viewpoint?

> If Anne Catherick had not died when she did, what should I have done? I should, in that case, have assisted worn-out Nature in finding permanent repose. I should have opened the doors of the prison of Life, and have extended to the captive (incurably inflicted in mind and body both) a happy release …
>
> On a calm revision of all the circumstances – is my conduct worthy of any serious blame? Most emphatically 'No!' Have I not carefully avoided exposing myself to the odium of committing unnecessary crime? With my vast resources in chemistry, I might have taken Lady Glyde's life. At immense personal sacrifice I followed the dictates of my own ingenuity, my own humanity, my own caution, and took her identity instead. Judge me by what I might have done. How comparatively innocent! How indirectly virtuous I appear in what I really did!

Commentary

Fosco is admitting that:

■ although he did not need to kill Anne Catherick, who died naturally, he would have done so

■ he stole Laura's identity.

His defence is:

■ even if he had killed her, Anne's death would not have been murder but a kind of euthanasia

■ he could have killed Laura but did not.

Collins gives Fosco a remarkably persuasive tongue, and this is an outrageous example of special pleading, so outrageous that you may see the effect as black comedy. He justifies his attitude to Anne through figurative language. He first refers to her death as rest – 'repose' – then develops the image of life as a prison with the words 'captive' and 'release'. The idea is that he would have conferred a benefit on Anne by murdering her, setting her free from life.

The second paragraph here uses exaggerated **rhetorical** patterning. He asks two questions, 'is my conduct worthy of serious blame?' and 'Have I not carefully avoided exposing myself to the odium of committing unnecessary crime?', then supplies the answers himself, directly appealing to the reader to give judgement on his side. In both cases he is emphatic that he is innocent because his actions might have been even worse. The threefold patterning of 'my own ingenuity, my own humanity, my own caution' is a well-known persuasive device (especially in political speeches). It pleases the ear as well as driving the idea home through emphasis.

Using emotive terms, Fosco even has the audacity to claim virtue and innocence for his actions. You will be glad to know that justice catches up with him before the end of the novel.

In analytical work, you should not speculate on what might happen outside the account given in the original text, but creative work is different. Philip Marlowe is attractive to women; would there be any possibility of a brief encounter between him and Adrienne Fromsett? Can you imagine a British Holden Caulfield spending time in London?

In Chapter 15 you will find an example of creative writing coursework that challenges the original point of view, in the piece entitled 'Mrs Brooker Bites Back'.

You might well think about other narratives from a different perspective. Some ways in which a piece of coursework might challenge the point of view of the set text could be:

■ Friday's view of Robinson Crusoe

■ Sally's view of Holden Caulfield after their date in Chapter 17 of *The Catcher in the Rye*

■ the British prisoners' view of Jim in *Empire of the Sun*

■ a political attack on socialism, in reply to George Orwell

■ Fanny Thornton's opinion of Margaret Hale in *North and South*

■ Degarmo's account of the emotional pressures on him in *The Lady in the Lake*.

Key terms

Rhetorical: using language persuasively in order to influence the opinions and behaviour of an audience.

Link

See page 79 for an example of coursework which deliberately challenges the original point of view.

13 Finding opportunities for creative work in different genres

Every text is related to other texts and displays genre characteristics. As you will know already, plots can be adapted in many different ways. The same basic material may be shaped into a variety of new formats: lengthened or shortened; made simpler or more complicated for a different audience or method of publication.

This chapter covers:

■ more possible approaches in planning creative writing coursework

■ the variety of genres suitable for new texts.

Practical activity

To understand how easy it is to adapt material to different genres, take a familiar nursery rhyme – 'Jack and Jill', for instance – and rewrite it as:

■ a text message from Jill to her friend

■ a play for children – all in dialogue

■ an accident report for an injury claim.

As well as changing the point of view, there are various other lines of approach that you might find useful in planning your creative writing coursework:

■ you can expand on the original narrative by introducing relevant extra material

■ you can rework the text in a different genre or for a different audience

■ you can exploit the setting, such as further details of plot

■ you can use a combination of these.

Your new text can be written for a reading audience or it can be in the form a text for spoken delivery. Remember that your work **must** reflect the set theme, however. For example, set themes for *The Adventures of Huckleberry Finn* and *The Catcher in the Rye* might be 'escape' or 'the hero's view of women'. A piece of coursework that did not reflect this would not fulfil the brief.

Monologues, letters, diaries, speeches, newspaper reports, play scripts – all these can give you an opportunity to show your understanding of the set texts in a creative way. Many of the texts have already been made into films; you could try writing your own original film script for part of the book you are studying. Because this is an integrated course, you will find material that you studied in Unit 1 and the Anthology highly relevant here. You might want to use the formats of other types of non-fictional document – for example, guidebooks – to present adaptations of literary material.

Extra chapters, short stories and monologues

Most works of fiction have places where the narrative might be expanded with an extra chapter. If you make a brief plot summary of the novel you are studying, you may see where there are time gaps or places where information has been summarised by 'telling' rather than 'showing' the action. Extra chapters can be a good way of showing a sensitive understanding of the characterisation and style of the original. It is even possible to find extra material for some non-fiction, but this may need highly specialised research and is probably not advisable in creative writing coursework.

 **Examiner's tip**

You need to think carefully about your choice of genre. While there are many genres that you can choose from, there are also some that you cannot realistically use. For example, it is not possible to script a live interview with one of the characters. Sometimes students waste a lot of effort in writing things that look like transcripts, complete with hesitations and false starts. There is no point in doing this; a conventional play would be much better.

Link

Chapter 15 includes a piece of coursework giving a model of a text that would stand alone. See page 76.

Key terms

Monologue: a text in which there is a single speaker.

Link

For the opening of Mr Fairlie's narrative see page 14.

You might choose to present the extra material as a short story complete in itself. Whereas an extra chapter is likely to lead on to the rest of the work, a short story might be constructed so that it would stand alone, in itself complete, even though clearly related to the original. Short stories are generally structured so that they have a limited number of characters and lead up to a climax of some sort at the end.

A **monologue**, by definition, is the voice of one speaker. However, it may contain reports of conversations with others. It has to create the character of the speaker as it goes along, as well as giving information, so it has to imply his or her attitudes to events. The main challenge is finding a suitable voice for the speaker because you have to create the character through the medium of speech. There are many different ways of doing this.

Do you remember the selfish and ridiculous Mr Fairlie in *The Woman in White*? Here is a little more of his narrative as a reminder.

'The last annoyance that has assailed me is the annoyance of being called on to write this Narrative. Is a man in my state of wretched nervousness capable of writing narratives? When I put this extremely reasonable objection, I am told that certain serious events relating to my niece have happened within my experience, and that I am the fit person to describe them on that account. I am threatened if I fail to exert myself in the manner required, with consequences which I cannot so much as think of without perfect prostration. There is really no need to threaten me. Shattered by my miserable health and my family troubles, I am incapable of resistance. If you insist, you take unfair advantage of me, and I give way immediately.'

Commentary

Fairlie is passive and reluctant. His focus in life is narrow. He has been 'required' to comment on events and is resisting hard. Fairlie's narrative repeats the pronoun 'I' a great deal to stress his selfishness. He presents himself as a victim, stressing his 'wretched nervousness', 'perfect prostration' and 'miserable health'. The jerky sentences suggest petulance.

Critical response activity

Here is a short extract from a different context completely, Marlow's narrative in *Heart of Darkness*, the novel that is paired with *Blood River* in your selection of set texts.

How does Conrad create the narrator's character here?

'Now when I was a little chap I had a passion for maps. I would look for hours at South America, or Africa, or Australia, and lose myself in all the glories of exploration. At that time there were many blank spaces on the earth, and so when I saw one that looked particularly inviting on the map (but they all look that) I would put my finger on it and say, When I grow up I will go there … But there was one yet – the biggest, the most blank so to speak – that I had a hankering after.

'True, by this time it was not a blank space any more. It had got filled since my boyhood with rivers and lakes and names. It had ceased to be a blank space of delightful mystery – a white patch for a boy to dream gloriously over. It had become a place of darkness. But there was in it one river especially, a mighty big river, that you could see on the map, resembling an immense snake uncoiled, with its head in the sea, its body at rest curving afar over a vast country, and its tail lost in the depths of the land. And as I looked at the map of it in a shop window, it fascinated me as a snake would a bird – a silly little bird.'

Commentary

Marlow is an active character, with the whole world as his field of interest. He is a visionary with an inner compulsion to investigate 'a place of darkness', to make comparisons and explore resonances. Conrad's framework narrator tells us that to Marlow 'the meaning of an episode was not inside like a kernel but outside, enveloping the tale which brought it out only as a glow brings out a haze'.

While Marlow conveys a sense of impending evil, he conveys it through figurative language, first in the way the 'white patch' of his boyhood has become the threatening 'place of darkness', then in the simile of the snake. The snake suggests both the shape of the river on the map and a dangerous predator. The narrator is drawn in by his fascination with the river, as a 'silly little bird' cannot resist the fatal attraction of the snake.

In both the above accounts the speaker is discussing his motivations, but the voices could not be more different in characterisation and style. Monologues may be serious or comic, straightforward or ironic, whatever the writer wishes.

> **AQA** Examiner's tip
>
> While monologues need to create a distinctive voice, it is a mistake to write in a mock historical style or in any non-standard form of language that does not come naturally to you. Above all, the voice has to be convincing.

Practical activity

Make a list of minor characters in the texts you have been studying and see how many of them might have a distinctive point of view about the events they witness. You might also suggest any actions they might take.

If you decide to write something from the point of view of a minor character, skim-read through the text and make notes before you start planning your actual piece. You can put sticky notes in the relevant pages of the book, or keep a list of references, but remember to write the page number of each reference so that you can find it again easily.

Letters and diaries

Letters and diaries are often good forms to choose because they give you a definite point in time to work from and this focus helps you sort out the relevant information. You have an upper limit of 850 words, but this could be divided into several short letters or diary entries if you write economically, giving you space to develop the characterisation a little. Blogs are another format that gives you similar opportunities.

Layout is relatively simple to manage. Letters need no more than an address and date at the top and an appropriate **salutation** and signature, although you might have to give some thought to the way characters would address each other in the period context. Nineteenth-century writers generally use more formal styles than we do; it is common for friends, and even husbands and wives, to address one another by their surname.

> **Key terms**
>
> **Salutation:** the opening of a letter, that usually says 'Dear ...'.

These genres closely resemble monologues because they are first-person narratives. They too need to convey the character of the writer, implying his or her attitudes and values as the writing proceeds.

In *Testament of Youth* Vera Brittain quotes her own diaries and letters to give variety and authenticity to her narrative. Here is part of a letter to her mother, written while she was a nurse at Camberwell, which relates how the hospital was told to expect a rush of wounded soldiers. It records facts, but it also conveys a strong sense of personal involvement. Graphic phrases like 'terrific tearing about' add liveliness to the scene.

> This afternoon … the hospital was warned to get ready for 150 patients, 50 officers and 100 men. We had not really that much accommodation for officers, so all the patients from one of the surgical wards in the College were transferred into one of the new huts and their ward made into an officers' ward. There was terrific tearing about all afternoon and everyone available was sent for to help haul mattresses, trollies and patients about … When I came off duty to-night the convoy had not yet arrived but was expected any hour. We were all warned by Matron to-night that very busy and strenuous days are ahead of us, and all our own arrangements must go quite on one side for the time being.

■ Critical response activity

To illustrate the range of possible effects further, here is part of a long fictional letter taken from *North and South*. It is essentially a business letter from Mr Bell, making arrangements for Margaret Hale after her father's death.

How does Gaskell convey a sense of personal relationship between Mr Bell and Margaret?

> MY DEAR MARGARET: – I did mean to have returned to Milton on Thursday, but unluckily it turns out to be one of the rare occasions when we, Plymouth Fellows, are called upon to perform any kind of duty, and I must not be absent from my post … You know, or if you don't, your poor father did, that you are to have my money and goods when I die. Not that I mean to die yet; but I name this just to explain what is coming. These Lennoxes seem very fond of you now; and perhaps may continue to be; perhaps not. So it is best to start with a formal agreement; namely, that you are to pay them two hundred and fifty pounds a year, as long as you and they find it pleasant to live together. (This, of course, includes Dixon; mind you don't be cajoled into paying any more for her.) Then you won't be thrown adrift, if some day the captain wishes to have his house to himself, but you can carry yourself and your two hundred and fifty pounds off somewhere else; if, indeed, I have not claimed you to come and keep house for me first. Then, as to dress, and Dixon, and personal expenses, and confectionery (all young ladies eat confectionery till wisdom comes by age), I shall consult a lady of my acquaintance, and see how much you will have from your father before fixing this. Now, Margaret, have you flown out before you have read this far, and wondered what right an old man has to settle your affairs so cavalierly? I make no doubt you have …

Commentary

The salutation sets the tone, because 'My dear Margaret' is intimate. (Terms of address were much more formal in the nineteenth century than we are used to.) Mr Bell can use Margaret's forename because he is her godfather, effectively taking the place of her dead father here.

The letter echoes the speaking voice in the use of elisions such as 'don't' and 'won't', and in informal, colloquial phrases like 'These Lennoxes', 'mind you don't' and 'carry yourself … off'. Mr Bell is deliberately making light of all the financial details by touches of humour such as 'all young ladies eat confectionery'. At the end of this extract, he anticipates her possible objections and deals with them.

Mr Bell occupies relatively little space in the novel as a whole, but he is important to the plot. At this point in the novel, Margaret Hale's social position is transformed as she becomes an independent heiress because of Bell's promised legacy. Gaskell's letter here essentially fills in background to this change of status. It is the style she adopts in this letter, creating an affectionate relationship between her characters, that makes the plot plausible.

If you look carefully, there are a number of points in the range of set texts where letters are mentioned but not actually quoted. You could supply one of these, perhaps with a reply.

Speeches

Speeches for formal occasions are often written out as complete texts, although they are delivered orally. We are all familiar with the idea that public figures have speech writers who provide the actual text for them to read off a paper or an autocue. Speeches delivered from notes may be written down in a complete form afterwards; this applies even to some weddings or funerals, where there may be a wider audience than the immediate guests who are interested in the occasion.

You will be aware of some of the common techniques of rhetorical speech and the features it tends to use, such as repetition, patterns of three, alliteration, striking imagery and so on.

A new political speech based on *The Road to Wigan Pier* might go something like this:

Theme: social class

Britain is in a mess. We live under a morally bankrupt system, and it is getting worse.

What is the alternative?

Everyone with elementary common sense, everyone who understands the meaning of poverty, everyone who has a hatred of tyranny, should see that socialism offers us a way out.

Under our capitalist system, any project that doesn't offer fast and fat profits to the private sector is rapidly rejected. Enterprises for the common good fall by the wayside. The gap between rich and poor widens into a chasm.

In the name of justice and liberty, we must have change.

Depending on the set theme, there may be various opportunities for speeches or lectures. These could range from serious speeches on conditions in the Congo or feminism, to entertaining ones at an engagement or christening party.

Newspaper and magazine articles

Articles in the press use styles you will be familiar with from Unit 1 as well as from daily life. They are third-person accounts, and they need headlines, sometimes subheadings, and quotations. It is important to envisage the kind of audience you are writing for because local papers are different from national ones and different papers have very different levels of formality.

Vera Brittain quotes from newspapers to stress the impact of news from the battlefields of the First World War. The headlines are conspicuous:

> BRITISH OFFENSIVE BEGINS – OFFICIAL
> FRONT LINE BROKEN OVER
> 16 MILES
> FRENCH SHARE ADVANCE
> THE FIGHTING DEVELOPING IN
> INTENSITY

By no means, however, are all events that newspapers describe so important or dramatic. Local papers often carry personal interest stories, and the material that you can make into a letter would sometimes be equally effective as an article in a newspaper or magazine. The trick is to choose the right style for the right paper.

Emmeline Grangerford in *The Adventures of Huckleberry Finn* 'kept a scrapbook when she was alive, and used to paste obituaries and accidents and cases of patient suffering in it out of the *Presbyterian Observer*, and write poetry after them out of her own head'. Without sharing Emmeline's rather specialised taste in news, readers of the Mississippi Valley local papers might still be very interested in:

- the disappearance and apparent death of Huck Finn
- the confidence tricks perpetrated by the duke and the king
- the progress of the feud between the Grangerfords and Shepherdsons.

Scripts

One way in which you might choose to adapt the material of your text in a different genre is by presenting it as a script. Remember, though, that what is being assessed here is your use of the English language in the particular genre you have chosen. Methods of presentation such as storyboards, which you may have come across in Media Studies, would not be appropriate here.

There are three common kinds of script, offering different problems and opportunities, and each with its own conventions. These are for:

- film or television
- radio
- stage plays.

If you look at a film script, you will probably notice the large number of short scenes and the high ratio of description to dialogue. Film is a very flexible medium and offers great opportunities for conveying information in visual form, but each shot has to be planned. Published scripts normally contain a good deal of description for this reason, but less dialogue than a stage play. The number of characters and locations is limited only by the budget.

Radio scripts can also use a large number of characters; actors will often double up in different parts by using different voices. You can use a narrator, although this is often a clumsy device in a play. If you want to avoid using a narrator, everything that the listener needs to understand has to be conveyed through the medium of sound. At the simplest level, to indicate that a character has arrived you need another character to greet him or her, or you might use sounds such as footsteps. The script has to indicate the use of fades, sound effects, music and so on.

Writing for the stage presents different challenges again. There will be much more dialogue in a play script than in one written for film or television. The script has to take into account the kind of theatrical space available, and limit the number of actors. Even if a play had several scene changes, there are normally fewer sets than in a film. However, in both plays and films characters have to make realistic entrances and exits to the location where the scene is set.

Non-fiction formats

In Unit 1 you will have studied the language of some shorter non-fiction texts. There are a few genres, such as guidebooks, that can be exploited for interesting creative writing.

Critical response activity

Some of the information in the following text is borrowed from *The Woman in White*. What features of the following imaginary guide to Limmeridge Hall seem characteristic of guide material in general?

On your left as we leave the Small Drawing Room is the Picture Gallery. Light levels are kept low in here to protect the Rembrandt etchings displayed in the walnut cabinet against the far wall. The dark red damask on the walls is the original.

The fine Madonna and Child by Raphael, acquired by Mr Frederick Fairlie in 1830, is the best example of the artist's work still in private hands. Mr Fairlie was a notable collector of antique coins as well as artworks, but most of these had to be sold some years ago in order to raise money to maintain the building.

A particular feature of this room is the charming collection of watercolours of Cumbria, painted by Mr Walter Hartright, the great-grandfather of the present owner, as a gift for his wife soon after they came to live at Limmeridge. The portrait of Mr Hartright himself which hangs to the left of the marble fireplace is by G. F. Watts. A portrait of Laura Hartright and her two young sons, Walter and John, painted by Millais, balances it on the right.

Commentary

This text creates the scene as if the reader was there, giving directions to left and right of the room and of the fireplace. The description has visual elements, such as the colour of the walls, intended to make it realistic. It points out the history of Limmeridge House as though the events related in *The Woman in White* were in the distant past and the pictures are all that remains.

Link

For an example of possible layout for a film script see page 74.

Some of the objects mentioned, such as the etchings, are taken from details in the novel itself, but other details, such as the portraits of Laura and Walter, have been added as the result of background research. Millais and Watts were producing portraits of the rich and famous at an appropriate time.

Similarly, other locations could be the basis for creative work. It is easy to imagine a theme park based on *Robinson Crusoe*, for instance, where young visitors are allowed to pet the goats and asked not to give unsuitable food to the tame parrots. John Thornton's premises in Milton might end up as an industrial museum. However, the work must be connected to the set theme. These suggestions might be appropriate if the theme for *North and South* was 'industrial conflict' or if that for *Robinson Crusoe* was 'conquering the environment'.

14 Writing for a different audience

Audiences may be specialist in a number of ways. They can be defined by readership, such as age or gender, or by special interests, such as art, geography or criminology. To take a rather extreme example, you might imagine Holden Caulfield's psychiatrist writing up his case notes in a professional journal.

A text often has more than one audience, and this is particularly true of anything you write that will be formally assessed. Apart from the primary audience, you are also writing for your teacher, who will be looking out for your ability to be creative and accurate in the use of written English, and for suitably chosen material.

Students who are writing about lowlife characters sometimes ask whether it is acceptable to use swear words for realism. The answer is that you should write what is appropriate for the subject, genre and audience you have selected, bearing in mind good taste. There is no point in giving unnecessary offence. Always check with your teacher if you are unsure about the suitability of what you have in mind.

One way that you might adapt material for a different audience is by writing a text for children. There have been a number of adaptations of *Robinson Crusoe* published for this audience, but writing for children is never a soft option and to do it well involves a very skilled use of language. The first problem is that the term 'children' covers such a wide range of different people, with different abilities and interests at different ages. You would have to define a specific age group and do some basic research in the kind of literature that that age group usually reads before you can begin.

The most suitable texts for young readers, like *The Adventures of Huckleberry Finn*, are often inventive and witty. They work on a number of levels and have a great deal to offer adults as well. In Chapters 5 and 6, you looked at some of the philosophical and moral issues raised in the course of Huck's adventures, which imply a sophisticated understanding on the part of the audience.

Adaptations

Many novels have been adapted either for the stage or for film. You may well have seen a film version of the texts you are studying, and noted how it differs from the prose text. Often readers feel that something is lost in the film version, because it has to be simplified, as films can only take up a relatively short time, whereas novels take several hours to read. The outcome is not always disappointing, however. Sometimes a good film can sharpen up a novel, and some actors can get the best out of even unpromising material.

An adaptation from novel to film script has to convey visual information that will focus the narrative for the viewer. This is only part of the process of making a film, of course, but it gives the director material to work on.

This chapter covers:

- different kinds of audience
- different registers of language appropriate for the audience
- adaptations.

■ Critical response activity

Here is an adaptation of a scene near the beginning of *Empire of the Sun*.
■ What is the primary audience for this text?
■ What visual motifs are important?
■ What features of **graphology** and language strike you?

Theme: Danger

Scene 4. Interior. Dr Lockwood's house

(A fancy-dress party. The camera picks up different elaborate costumes, including Jim's father as a pirate. A general hum of conversation among the guests. Chinese servants with impassive faces serve trays of drinks. We follow Jim weaving in and out among the groups of adults, largely ignored, playing with his balsa model plane. Shot through the window of planes passing overhead.)

Woman: *(Looking at passing planes)* Tell me Dr Lockwood, what is the latest on the Japanese advance? Have you heard anything we don't already know?

Host: Nothing good I'm afraid. *(She looks anxious.)* Here, I'll put the radio on for you, if you like, and see if there is anything we don't already know.

(Radio crackles as he switches it on. Adults gather round the set. View of their backs as they listen intently, drinks and conversation abandoned. Jim melts away through an open window, making his plane fly in front of him.)

Scene 5. Exterior. Hungjao disused airfield

(We follow Jim, still flying his plane, running through a cultivated garden. He dodges through a gap in the fence, and out onto an overgrown concrete road. He crosses another fence and ditch, the perimeter of an airfield, and launches his toy plane high into the air. It comes down beside a derelict Japanese plane abandoned at the end of a runway, half hidden by undergrowth, and Jim scrambles after it.)

Scene 6. Interior. The party

(Conversation resumes as the adults switch off the radio and turn away with anxious faces. Jim's father looks round and misses him. Through the window he sees the boy in the far distance; his face expresses horror as we see him scramble out and follow Jim's direction.)

Scene 7. Exterior. Hungjao airfield

(Cut to the trees and undergrowth round the wreck of the plane. As Jim rushes forwards towards where his toy lies, a Japanese soldier steps out of the shadows close to him. Jim freezes. He and the soldier look at one another for a long moment. Close up of the soldier's face. Cut to a shot of Jim's father rushing through the gap in the fence. He sees the soldier and pretends to call casually.)

Father: Jamie … We're all waiting … Jamie, you're missing the fireworks.

(Father bows to the soldier and holds out his hand to Jim, who also bows politely and backs away. As they turn away we see more soldiers advancing slowly across the airfield.)

Jim:	My plane's down there.
Father:	We'll leave it for the soldiers – finders keepers.
Jim:	Like kites?
Father:	That's it.
Jim:	He wasn't very angry.
Father:	It looks as if they're waiting for something to happen.
Jim:	The next war?
Father:	*(Pause)* I don't suppose so.

(No one follows them. As they reach the concrete road, Jim's father helps him through the fence, then suddenly hugs him tight. They increase their pace back towards the house. In the distance the party is breaking up and cars are leaving. More planes pass overhead, coming in low.)

Commentary

The primary audience here is the director and the rest of the team making the film, so the script concentrates on action and description. There are far more elaborate descriptions of the scene than you would expect in a play script, and less dialogue. There are references to what the camera is following. Some film scripts are also published for a wider audience, and may be read like a play.

An important visual motif here is the plane. Jim's balsa wood model plane leads him into the airfield. The real planes in the sky signal imminent danger.

There is no absolutely standard way of setting out film scripts. If you look at published scripts you will see variations, but obviously the text must distinguish between directions and dialogue. Here the material that will be presented visually is set in italics, while the dialogue is in a Roman typeface, with the speaker's name at the side as it would be in a play.

The writer has taken most of the dialogue directly from the novel, because it is brief and concentrated. This is invariably not the case; sometimes the talk needs adaptation for the new medium, especially if the original is an old text.

The main problem with adaptations of this sort is that they tend to reduce the original. The example above is rather flat in effect, especially when compared with Ballard's novel. Obviously the amount of material that can be handled within the coursework brief is limited, so choosing suitable scenes that are reasonably self-contained and make a dramatic impact is important.

Not all adaptations stick as closely to the source material as this. The most famous film version of *Heart of Darkness* is *Apocalypse Now*, which transfers the scene of the action to Vietnam.

15 How will the creative writing coursework be assessed?

Criteria for assessment

To help you understand the assessment criteria, here is a brief reminder of the qualities on which creative writing coursework will be judged:

- interest and originality
- relevance to the set theme
- appropriate use of genre
- quality of written English.

Remember that this task tests all the Assessment Objectives, especially AO4:

Demonstrate expertise and creativity in using language appropriately for a variety of purposes and audiences, drawing on insights from literary and linguistic studies.

The examples of possible coursework responses given below show three different kinds of reaction to the same pair of texts, *North and South* and *The Road to Wigan Pier*. They also illustrate the same theme, social class, but with different levels of success.

The best scripts will be interesting to read and will show originality by adding to our understanding of their source material. In this task the writer's own command of written language is obviously very important.

You have an opportunity here to use some of the skills and techniques that you have observed in professional writers' work throughout Chapters 1–10 of this book. This is also a good place to show creative understanding of the context of the texts you have studied and to use information you have gained through background research.

Sample response A: North and South

Theme: social class

The Little Companion

Establishes the atmosphere	It is only October, but the air is cold and a thin fog hangs over the London streets. In the dull grey afternoon light a cab deposits Richard Hale and his daughter at the door of 96 Harley Street. Margaret Hale wriggles down from the cab and stares up at the red brick building, four storeys high.
Accurate detail from text, followed by evidence of background research	

'The street's like a canyon, Papa,' she whispers, as a smart footman opens the door and deals with their luggage. 'Why are there no trees or gardens?'

Use of dialogue to set the scene	'The trees are in the squares and in Regent's Park, my love,' her father reassures her. 'Your aunt Shaw will take you in her carriage, I'm sure.'

Because of the fog, the gas is already lit in the drawing room where Mrs Shaw is waiting for them. She is a pretty woman in her thirties. The gaslight makes her silk gown shimmer. Margaret, who is used to candles at home, sees the lights, smells the scent of hothouse roses in the room, and knows that she is in a foreign world.

Use of sense impressions appropriate to the situation

'Maria sends her love and her apologies,' Richard tells his sister-in-law. She's unable to get away just at the moment, and I must return to my parish tomorrow, too.' He does not add that his wife refused to come because of clothes. A new gown, cut with wide sloping shoulders and a pointed waist, like the one her sister is now wearing, would have made her eager for the trip.

Further evidence of research into the context

Good-natured and easy-going, Mrs Shaw understands nothing of this; she only ever sees the pleasant side of things. She married an old man for his money, acted the role of good wife while he lived, and has enjoyed a life of elegant indulgence, leisure and pleasure, since his death.

Neat phrasing

She rings for a footman.

'Tell Newton to bring Miss Edith down to meet her cousin,' she orders, then turns to Margaret. 'I do hope you'll be happy with us,' she tells the child. A silky lapdog clambers up onto her knee and she pets it absent-mindedly. 'Edith will be so glad to have someone to play with and share her lessons.'

A possible parallel between Margaret and the dog, as pets

Edith appears – a picture-book vision of blonde curls and white muslin. She holds out her hand politely to her uncle, then takes possession of Margaret with a confident hug and kiss, leaving her cousin pleased but a little alarmed at this unexpected petting.

'Don't they look pretty together,' says Mrs Shaw. 'Margaret has your dark hair, such a sweet contrast.' She is much too polite even to hint at a further contrast in dress. Margaret has a neat darn in the heel of one stocking, and her frock has been let down at the hem. The child must have some nice things tomorrow, she thinks.

Details relevant to the theme of social status

'Take Margaret up to the nursery and show her your dolls, Edith,' she says, 'until Newton brings your tea. Margaret must be hungry after her long journey.'

This moment of separation is so casual. Margaret has always shared meals with her parents. Her father nods weakly, and Edith leads her away, up and up it seems, a great distance to the top of the house where the servants sleep and Edith keeps whole regiments of dolls at her command.

The character of Edith developed

Dinner downstairs is a quiet affair; only Edith's governess shares the meal, a small, thin woman with greying hair.

'Is your daughter fond of music, Mr Hale?' she asks. 'Edith already plays very well and practises every day.'

'I believe she likes to sing and her mother has taught her to play a little.'

'Then she will enjoy our music. Edith will love to have an audience.'

Dialogue gives further evidence of Margaret's dependent position

Richard refuses the offer of wine and goes straight into the drawing room with his sister-in-law. She pours him coffee.

'We are so glad to have Margaret,' she says. 'Edith is a dear little thing, but she is growing up fast and an only child needs a companion of the right sort, don't you think? A few years and she will be going to parties and balls. It'll be just like when Maria and I lived with Sir John at Beresford Court. You lead such a quiet life now you've probably forgotten. Do you remember the time we were all at Torquay?'

Further mention of their relative social positions to reinforce the point

'Of course. But Maria and I do dine with the bishop every year,' says Richard defensively, 'and we are friendly with several families in the neighbourhood.'

Mrs Shaw changes the subject.

'Shall we go up and see if Margaret is asleep?' she asks.

They climb up to the nursery where Margaret, who has been waiting, is tucked up in a snowy white bed. She hears them coming, but knows she is supposed to be asleep and so pretends, wiping away a tear with a corner of the sheet.

'I know you'll take good care of her,' says Richard.

'Of course, and Edith will be so pleased.'

As they disappear downstairs, Margaret bursts into real sobs.

'Hush,' says the nursery maid who comes in to see her, 'you'll wake Miss Edith.'

> Summarises Margaret's helpless position

> A quotation from Gaskell's text which fits in well and provides a moving climax to the story

Commentary

This piece takes as its starting point a quotation from the novel and elaborates on it, leading up to Margaret's sobs and the nursery maid's response as the main point of the story. It is sometimes dangerous to use direct quotations like this, but here the dialogue gives a poignant climax to the series of events. The script is original in that it adds to our understanding of Margaret's position and feelings.

The bias here is a little different from Gaskell's text because we feel sorry for Margaret throughout, whereas *North and South* stresses the way she adapts to her role in the Shaw household when she is older. It is a valid interpretation of the theme of social class, however. Margaret's position in the house is that of poor relation. She is there to be useful to her rich aunt and cousin, although they treat her kindly.

The writer has used the whole of the word allowance, but has not exceeded it, and has paced the material accordingly. Not everything in the new text is taken directly from the novel. There is evidence of background research in the descriptions of Harley Street in the 1840s and of early Victorian fashion. Where information has been taken from different parts of the novel, it is well assimilated. For example, the detail about Mrs Hale refusing to visit her sister because of her clothes is taken from a different family occasion, but it seems plausible here.

The opening creates an appropriate atmosphere for the story, stressing the chilly surroundings. Dialogue dramatises the scene, showing us the action as it unfolds. The writer also makes use of sense impressions, such as the gaslight and the scent of roses in Mrs Shaw's drawing room. The repetition of Edith's name stresses the way Margaret is seen as dependent on her and in an inferior position. There is even a possible suggestion that Margaret's position is parallel to that of the lapdog or the 'regiments' of dolls.

This script shows a creative response to the set text, with an original interpretation of material both from the novel and from research. Its expression is clear and accurate. It should achieve a good mark.

AQA Examiner's tip

When you use information from the set texts to create a new document, great tact is needed if you lift whole sentences from your source material. Occasionally you can use the original dialogue to good effect, but sometimes it will seem odd in the context of a different style. Much of the time it is better to make notes, and then put these into your own words.

Sample response B: The Road to Wigan Pier

Theme: social class

Mrs Brooker Bites Back

Chap named Orwell? Yes, I remember him, tall miserable-looking chap, always moaning, never satisfied. Him and that other chap from down South who left – little Cockney he was – traveller for a cigarette firm – he complained. He stood there in me own kitchen and said the place stank! That Orwell laughed. No one else ever complained. Mr Reilly been here for months, happy as Larry. That's right, one of them stuck-up moaners – You do your best for people and they treat you like dirt.

> Creates the effect of a conversation with the reader; gives physical detail of Orwell's appearance

> Establishes a viewpoint, challenging Orwell's version

He was round here snooping, making some sort of notes, hanging round the place all the time looking miserable. Me back's that bad I have to stop on the settee in the living room day and night – can't manage the stairs for the pain – and there he was giving me dirty looks all the time, never a 'How are you Mrs Brooker?' or 'Can I pass you something?' He just looks me up and down. Most of our gentlemen goes out in the day time. If they've not got work they go and improve themselves in the public library like Joe, but not this Orwell chap. He was 'arranging to visit some coal mines,' he says. What for I don't know. My George was a miner till he got laid off two years since – he can tell you a coal mine ain't no place for visitors.

> Gives a plausible explanation for her behaviour as an invalid

So he's hanging round all the time, four solid meals a day while he's doing his arranging. It does seem 'ard, don't it now. You do your best for people, four square meals a day, all good food, bacon for breakfast, pie and potatoes and pudding for dinner – all out of the shop, lodgers gets the same as the customers do – a good strong brew at tea time and supper on top of that. I had a gentleman say to me last week, 'Mrs Brooker, I always enjoy your suppers – crackers and Lancashire cheese with a bit of pickle to top it off – you can't beat it.' But like I say, this Mr Orwell, he's always after the food, always trying to get George let him cut his own bread and butter, so's he can get a bit more all the time I reckon. And there's him hanging round this place sneering, superior like, all for his pound a week what he's paid for his board.

> A direct quotation as reported by Orwell

> Creates character by the use of reported speech within the monologue

> Explains why Mr Brooker always insists on handling the bread, one of Orwell's criticisms

We give value, we do. Of course not all our gentlemen is on full board. There's a couple of pensioners up the top of the house only pays half that. They ain't got it you see, so they pays ten shillings and we don't make hardly nothing out of that but they still gets the use of the kitchen fire to make themselves a bit of toast if they want to, and the use of the bathroom.

With me being stuck downstairs I get to see and hear a lot around meal times, and that Orwell he didn't half talk daft. I heard him giving Mr Reilly the low-down on this house in his posh accent. 'And that room we sleep in,' he says, 'ought to be the drawing room.' Drawing room! We don't do no drawing. It's hard enough keeping the place going as it is, with our Lily always up to the eyes with all the washing. Me other daughter's at Canada, but our Frank's wife Lily she helps out a bit, then there's Emmie, our Fred's girl, she comes round in the evening and knocks off a few dishes. Otherwise with me on me back it's me husband what has to do everything – get the froze up from the cellar, mind the shop, peel the spuds, do the rooms out. It's no life for a man what used to be a miner, but there's no work round here so we does the best we can with the tripe and the lodgers.

> Relevant to the theme of social status

> Presumably the writer intends this as a joke, but it does not quite work

> Some information about the Brooker family invented, expanding on details in the original text

Use of irony

And another thing – he was always wanting baths, even first thing in the morning. Had a thing about dirt, he did – and him wanting to go down the pit! You'd think he'd never seen a chamber pot in his life where he come from, the way he looks at George when he empties the slops. I've seen plenty of better gentlemen than him in my time, commercial gentlemen and artistes from the theatre and them as plays the pubs. But we don't seem to get no customers in the shop nowadays, so we 'as to do our best with the lodgers, like. It does seem 'ard, don't it now?

Commentary

This script has a balance of strengths and weaknesses. The writer has fulfilled the brief, kept to the right length and shows detailed knowledge of the text. She has been moderately adventurous in the writing, but has failed to be convincing in the use of language.

Orwell's disgusting portrait of the Brooker household at the beginning of *The Road to Wigan Pier* is a strong, detailed attack. The writer has been able to pick up the details and use them in reverse, to excuse Mrs Brooker and attack Orwell, bringing out the set theme of social class very well. The monologue creates the scene in the Brooker household for us. It is clear that the character of Mrs Brooker here is strongly aware that Orwell comes from a different world from hers, and to that extent the character is realistic and illustrates the set theme.

Although the script is quite well organised, it has some problems with the actual language, having been a little overambitious in the choice of this particular voice. It is very difficult to write convincing dialect, and this writer has not conveyed the sounds or grammar of Lancashire speech quite believably. It also has problems with the joke about the 'drawing room'. Humour is welcome in creative work, but it has to be appropriate. It is hard to believe that a real-life Mrs Brooker would actually make this mistake.

This script would be awarded a grade somewhere in the middle of the mark scale.

Sample response C: North and South

Theme: social class

MILTON TIMES

RIOTS AT MARLBOROUGH MILL

The script is full of errors of this kind, showing a lack of understanding of lexical functions or a lack of concern for technical accuracy

Soldiers had to be called yesterday when <u>their</u> was a riot at Marlborough Mill that belongs to Mr J. Thornton, the well-known mill owner in the town.

Trouble began when the men's Union called a strike. There where alot of work people in the town that did not agree with the wages going down because they needed the money so they went on a strike and

Too colloquial for a newspaper

Mr Thornton brought over a bunch of workers from Ireland to do the work for the people that where on strike. Not only men but women and children as well. They where very poor people who where willing

Faulty grammar

to work for anything. Yesterday afternoon a crowd came in the street outside Marlborough Mills that was very angry and started shouting and pushing outside the big gates of the mill and making a lot of noise

Wrong word

because they said Mr Thornton acted deceivingly bringing over the

Irish. They where rattling the gates like they where going to break them down and wanting to get at the Irish workers that was inside. Mr Thornton bolted the gates and sent for the soldiers but the crowd kept on making a big noise. Captain Hanbury, the man in charge of the soldiers told our reporter, 'It was a very dangerous situation. Fortune shinned on Mr Thornton that we got there in time.' Mr Thornton went inside but then he came out again and started to talk to the men to tell them to go away, the crowd saw it's chance to make a big row and got nasty. Then Miss Hale, aged 19, came out the door in front of the gates and started to shout at the crowd, 'Go – the soldiers are sent for – are coming. Go peaceably.'

> Wrong part of the verb, unclear spelling and syntax errors

> Shows awareness of the need to quote, but contains spelling error

> Has picked up a common feature of newspaper style here

> Victorian language seems out of place

Some of the rough lads in the crowd started taking off their heavy wooden clogs to throw them and Miss Hale threw herself round Mr Thornton's neck like she wanted to protect him or something. Then another lad threw a stone and it hit her on the head and there was blood running down her face and Mr Thornton went mad because they hit a woman and was out to get the Irish that he said was innocent. Then a lad in the crowd shouted, 'The stone were meant for thee but thou wert sheltering behind that woman,' but the crowd felt ashamed when Mr Thornton went back and then the soldiers was coming so they melted away straight off. Marlborough Mills is under police protection.

> Expression too colloquial

> Quotation slightly inaccurate

Miss Hale is reported to be OK but shocked. She went home after treatment.

> The expression 'OK' is too colloquial. Very uneven length of paragraphs

The strike is affecting other manufacturers in town that say they can't pay any more wages because of the price of cotton being gone up and sales not good and they wouldn't have any profits. Mr Thornton is the Union main target because he acted deceivingly and said the cuts in the wages to be expedient so as to preserve his own financial position.

> This paragraph attempts a more general view of the situation and could be developed

Commentary

This piece of coursework has a number of problems and needs extensive redrafting and correction before it can be confident of passing. The feature that needs most improvement is the writer's own use of English. It looks as though the draft has been put through a spellcheck at some stage, but this will not pick up errors such as 'where' for 'were', and 'their' for 'there'. A number of the mistakes and inelegancies have been underlined to draw attention to them.

The scene the writer has chosen is an important one, but as the script stands it has only marginal relevance to the set theme of social class. The conflict between mill owner and union could be made much more relevant with some changes of emphasis. At present the writer's main concern is just to tell the story of the riot, without any original insights. The final paragraph could be developed to bring out the theme, and so could the references to the poor Irish workers. The piece as it stands is short, only just over 500 words, so there would be plenty of space to do this.

The writing fails to be convincing as an article in a newspaper. The style is naïve, with limited vocabulary and poor control of paragraph and sentence structures. Paragraphs are very uneven in length and many sentences ramble. Rather than adding anything to our understanding, the writing here greatly diminishes the emotional effect of the scene as it was described in the novel. The writer could possibly claim that this is intended to be an objective report, but it still needs more perceptive comment on the events the *Milton Times* is describing and their significance. At present, it is largely a summary of material taken from a single chapter of *North and South*.

The writer is aware of some of the conventions of the newspaper genre. The piece has headlines and some direct speech. The two quotations from the novel, one where Margaret says 'Go peaceably' and, to a slightly lesser extent, the words from the man in the crowd who speaks dialect, seem incongruous in this context, however, especially since the quotation from Captain Hanbury is in a different style.

Practical activity

Put the second paragraph of this text into correct modern Standard English, keeping the basic information the same.

Recording planning

As part of your coursework you have to show evidence of planning. This is not assessed and can be a single handwritten A4 sheet. Its purpose is to show how you have approached the task. It will show that you have understood the original text you studied and the process you have been through in order to create a new one related to it.

You might mention what audience your creative writing coursework is intended for as part of this, and note in general terms the kind of adaptations you have made. Although you are not expected to produce a detailed commentary on your new text, you might note whether you have been able to try it out on its intended audience, and the effect of any feedback from this.

If you have used existing works as a model, or undertaken considerable internet research, you should give a reference to these sources.

The final stage

When you have written a draft of your coursework that you are satisfied with, and put it through the computer's spellcheck, wait a couple of days, then read it aloud to yourself. If you can read it to someone else who will help you with constructive criticism, that is even better. Does it sound right? You will probably find that you want to make small alterations even at this stage. Take care to double-check the spelling and punctuation. Spellings of names can be tricky and need extra care.

You do not have to submit any drafts for assessment, only the final version.

Finally, imagine yourself reading the work aloud to your teacher, whose responsibility it is to apply the assessment criteria and pass on your coursework marks to AQA. Would your teacher and the external moderator be convinced that this is your best work and that you have taken every care?

Type a neat title page for your work. Then hand it all in comfortably ahead of the deadline.

AQA Examiner's tip

Remember to keep back-up copies of your work at every stage. There is nothing more distressing than to find that your computer has crashed just before the deadline and you have no up-to-date copy.

Further reading

- Peter Boxall (ed.), *1001 Books You Must Read before You Die*, Cassell, 2006
- David Crystal, *The Story of English*, Penguin, 2005
- David Crystal, *A Little Book of Language*, Yale, 2010

Glossary

A

Autobiography: the story of a person's own life, written by himself or herself.

C

Colloquial: language that may be used in ordinary conversation but is not appropriate in formal or literary contexts.

Complex sentence: a sentence with two or more clauses linked by subordinating conjunctions such as 'which', 'while', 'where'.

Connotations: the associations that words evoke in the mind of the reader. For example, there is a difference between 'house', which suggests a building, and 'home', which suggests a place where people live.

D

Diachronic variation: the changes in language over time.

Dialect: a variety of a particular language characterised by distinctive features of accent, grammar and vocabulary, used by people from a geographical area or social group.

Dialogue: direct speech between two or more characters in a narrative. It normally imitates some but not all of the features of real-life talk.

E

Elision: the running together of words or the omission of parts of words – for example, 'don't' for 'do not' or 'y'know' for 'you know'.

Ellipsis: the omission of part of a sentence, which is then understood from the context. 'Hope you get well soon' is an example of ellipsis where the pronoun 'I' has been left out. An ellipsis is sometimes represented by three dots (...) to indicate the missing part of a sentence.

Epigram: a pithy saying or remark that sums up an idea.

Episode: a self-contained event that can be identified within the main sequence of events in the narrative.

Episodic: an episodic narrative consists of a series of events that do not overlap or affect each other – for example, the main character moves from place to place, having different adventures in each.

Etymology: the study of the origin and meaning of words.

F

Figurative language: language that makes an imaginative comparison between what the writer is describing and something else, so as to bring in a different set of connotations. For example, 'red as a rose' has quite different connotations from 'red as beetroot'. The common figures of speech are simile, metaphor and personification. They are often also referred to as 'imagery'.

G

Genre: a class or category of text with its particular conventions of language, form and structure – for example, short story, science-fiction novel, Shakespearean comedy.

Gothic horror: a style of fiction that stresses mystery and extreme emotional reaction.

Graphology: the layout of a text with use of such features as typeface.

I

Idiolect: the language characteristics of an individual speaker, including choice of vocabulary and idiom, grammar and pronunciation.

Imagery: see Figurative language.

Intertextuality: the way one text partly depends for its meaning on reference to another text.

Irony: a mismatch or discrepancy between what is written and what is actually meant – for example, where the reader makes a judgement of the narrator by using a different set of values or taking a different point of view.

M

Metaphor: an implied comparison, speaking of one action or thing as if it were another. For example, 'she flew down the road' does not literally mean that she took to the air, but that she moved fast.

Minor sentences: sentences without a verb, most commonly used in conversation.

Monologue: a text in which there is a single speaker.

N

Narrative: an account of connected events.

O

Omniscient narrator: a third-person point of view that allows an 'all-knowing' author to describe both outward details and a character's inner thoughts and feelings. Omniscient narrators can move freely between different characters and scenes, with full knowledge of everything that happens. They are able to comment on events and themes as well as describing them.

P

Pathetic fallacy: the literary technique of suggesting human states and emotions through the description of details such as landscape and weather. For example, a writer might use a dreary setting on a rainy day to suggest that a character is feeling sad. It is a 'fallacy' because inanimate surroundings cannot really respond to human feelings except in the imagination.

Personification: a specialised form of metaphor speaking of non-human things as if they were human – for example, 'the windows stared blankly'.

Picaresque: a novel that describes the adventures, usually comic, of a lively and resourceful hero on a journey. The name comes from the Spanish word *pícaro*, which means rascal.

Plot: the arrangement of narrative events in a story organised in such a way as to create links between them and maintain interest for the reader.

Protagonist: the leading character, or one of the major characters, in a literary text.

R

Register: a variety of language that is used for particular purposes or within a particular social context. Important features are how formal or how technical the expression is. For example, 'they ain't done nothing' is informal and comes from a spoken register; in a formal written register this is more likely to be 'they have not done anything'. 'A plane' is far less technical than 'a Fairchild Γ-227'.

Rhetorical: using language persuasively in order to influence the opinions and behaviour of an audience.

S

Salutation: the opening of a letter, that usually says 'Dear ...'.

Semantic field: a group of words within a text all relating to the same topic.

Simile: a direct comparison, usually introduced by 'like' or 'as' – for example, 'as quiet as a mouse'.

Symbol: an action or object that resonates beyond its literal meaning to represent a wider idea or concept.

Syntax: the linguistic term for the structure of sentences.

T

Taboo language: language considered offensive or improper to use, and therefore banned by some speakers.

Themes: major subjects in a text, often representing ideas that recur during the narrative.

Index

Key terms are in **bold**